A CUP OF COFF[barcode I0070026]
10 LEADING ATTORNEYS IN THE UNITED STATES

CONSTITUTIONAL CHAMPIONS SHARE THEIR
STORIES, EXPERIENCES, AND INSIGHTS

Judge Paul H. LaValle, Esq.
Randy Van Ittersum

Rutherford Publishing House
PO Box 969
Ramseur, NC 27316
www.RutherfordPublishingHouse.com

Cover photo: Roman Fedin (tai111)/Fotolia.com
Book layout/design: Richard E. Spalding

ISBN-10: 0692791531
ISBN-13: 978-0692791530

TABLE OF CONTENTS

ACKNOWLEDGEMENTS

We all want to thank our husbands and wives, fathers and mothers, and everybody who has played a role in shaping our lives and our attitudes.

To all the clients we've had the honor of working with, who shaped our understanding of the difficulty of this time for you and your families. It has been our privilege to serve each and every one of you.

INTRODUCTION

In my work, I often have occasion to read inspiring stories from some of the best professional people all around the country. I learn about their hopes, their dreams, their wins, and their losses. I always gather insights and generally develop a new appreciation for the class of folk whose walls are decorated with elegant degrees from esteemed universities around the world. I came to this book with my standard eager interest, but because it was a book about lawyers, I expected more of the usual "get it in writing" kind of advice we've all seen.

Contributing Author:
Randy Van Ittersum
Host & Founder – Business Leader Spotlight Show

Some believe it was William Shakespeare who first laid the groundwork for the "anti-barrister movement." Four hundred years ago in his play *Henry VI*, Shakespeare offered this prescription for improving the world: "First thing we do is kill all the lawyers." The Bard's position is extreme, of course, but some disdain for lawyers still persists today. We've all heard more than our share of jokes about lawyers. These stories paint pitiful caricatures of ambulance-chasing personal injury lawyers, and less-than-ethical shysters who feed from the bottom of the judicial pond. As you read this book, I expect those stereotypical visuals will dissipate as mine did.

LAWYERS ARE PEOPLE TOO

The attorneys whose stories populate the pages of this book are real people who give us a new perspective on why their profession is not only noble, necessary, and even constitutionally compulsory, but also how they make this world a more tender place. Surely you jest? Tenderness? Yes, tenderness. These learned men and women are renowned for their bitter battles in the modern-day coliseum we call a courtroom, but the batch of legal eagles whose stories reside herein do a marvelous job of addressing the "why" of it to the extent that I'm swayed to become a platinum member of the Barrister Booster Club.

I've always known that shrewd people can and have salvaged entire fortunes by having attorneys and accountants do their planning for them. As I read this book, though, I realize that even the modestly funded among us have need of and can claim those same victories. By careful planning and forward thinking, lawyers can eliminate contentious litigation later and actually take advantage of all the state laws about which we lay folk don't know. By employing their specialized learning of the intricacies of probate and estate laws, all the wealth a client has been able to amass—however great or small—can be safeguarded, nurtured, and passed on to the progeny as it was meant to be. It can also be safeguarded from greedy governments that would soak up any dollars left untended by those who simply had no idea of the consequences.

Who needs to read this book? Perhaps you are among the bright-eyed law students who pick up the books in this series as an introduction to sundry specialties within the law. If so, you will be especially pleased with the variety of perspectives offered between these covers. We give you a long look at Estate

Planning, Business Law, and International Law, along with new perspectives on Personal Injury, Medical Malpractice, Criminal Defense, and Family Law.

Should you strike out on your own, or join an established firm? Should you strive for a place in a high-volume firm, or do you want to fledge in a small firm where your experience is bound to be more extensive? You'll find suggestions and personal reflections on each here.

Here also, you will find valuable insight about how to grow your practice long before you even get that coveted Juris Doctorate. You will learn how to maximize your personal and private networks into one big referral-generating machine. You will be reminded how to use technology in order to make every moment of your time count for something, no matter where your travels take you. You'll learn about building relationships with your clients as well as your colleagues. You also will also learn the value of relentless learning and deliberate honing of your skills.

The depth of dedication and mission these men and women share belies the stereotypical image often foisted upon attorneys. Each of the practitioners within this book offers you a glimpse into the "fire in the belly" that marks a truly great attorney. They each talk about the resolve which fuels their own dedication. These people take the meaning of the word *ADVOCATE* to heart.

In this world, there are people who are honestly underdogs and must play David to the Goliath of gigantic corporations, insurance providers, pharmaceutical companies and, yes, even their own government. Lawyers, armed with an intimate knowledge of the law, step out to save those among us who are without adequate defenses.

These are the people who take giant tire companies and automakers to task for making decisions based upon money, not mortality. In the very recent past, corporate decisions have been made based on a scale that measures the cost of a product recall against the number of human deaths that could possibly occur as a result of a faulty device. It is in this same environment that we find factory and mine workers whose health and future happiness are subject to the decisions of corporate accountants who, so often, choose bigger profits over employee safety.

We hear the personal stories of the lawyers themselves, some of whom immigrated to this country as children with parents in search of a better life. Old-world values live on in these plain people who dedicate their careers to advocating for vulnerable others.

Whether you are a career lawyer or a convenience store clerk, there are lessons in this book for you. Beyond the remarkable dedication to their vocation, you will find among these pages solid business guidance. Each chapter has gems that can enrich your own career if you will put them to work. Consider the value of the others around you and act accordingly. Think about how you can improve your own community and elevate your place in society by being focused on what is the greater good. Learn the importance of developing a reputation for taking on the hard work—to even risk failure—because, after all, if you don't break eggs, you won't make many omelets.

The subjects of billing, client base cultivation, communication, and client expectation are also covered here. And there are lessons for us laypeople as well.

- Know that do-it-yourself legal documents and cyber lawyers can cost you far, far more than an hour with a flesh-and-blood attorney.

- There is misinformation on the Internet—yes. Really!

- Understand that postponing estate planning or the creation of your last will and testament can destroy the inheritance you planned to leave your children.

- Know that what you hear on television about "Tort Reform" may not be entirely true.

- Learn how you can protect your own constitutional rights.

Perhaps the most resounding of the admonitions in this book is the reminder that none of us knows it all. For my part, I realized that there are serious issues lurking in places I might never have expected to find them. For example, even if your aging parent seems well and intellectually sound, the split-second in which a stroke occurs can change everything forever. A little time spent with an Elder Law expert before the fact can help you avoid countless complications and difficulties in providing for the care of an aging parent. Knowing NOT to sign any offer from an insurance adjuster, no matter how attractive the amount may seem, until you've spoken with an attorney can ensure that your compensation is fair and just in the long term.

The lessons are many in "*A Cup of Coffee With 10 Leading Attorneys In The United States*," but the meaning is crystal clear. We no longer live in a world where a handshake can seal a deal. So, yes, get it in writing, but before you do, talk with somebody whose interest is in keeping you safe from yourself and the others who don't always have your best interests at heart.

Randy Van Ittersum
Host & Founder – Business Leader Spotlight Show

1

—

LEGACY LAWYER

by Judge Paul H. LaValle, Esq.

Judge Paul H. LaValle, Esq.
Law Office of Paul Houston LaValle
& Associates, PC
Houston, Texas
www.lavalle-law.com

Judge Paul Houston LaValle is a graduate of South Texas College of Law and specializes in product liability, personal injury, wrongful death, trucking accidents, aviation, DOSA and FSLA. The Law Office of Paul Houston LaValle & Associates, P.C. is based in Houston, Texas and focuses on product liability, commercial litigation, criminal defense, both "white collar" and "street" crimes, employment law, family law, military/veterans and other legal matters.

A lifelong resident of Galveston County, Texas, Judge Paul H. LaValle is the son of the elder Judge LaValle who also served the people of Texas. Judge LaValle is a Life Member of both the Million Dollar Advocates Forum and the Multi-Million Dollar Advocates Forum, both are among the most prestigious groups of trial lawyers in the United States. Membership in the association is limited to only about 4000 attorneys across the United States who have won million and multi-million dollar verdicts, awards and settlements. Recently, Judge LaValle was honored by being named as a National Advisor to the Association of Personal Injury Trucking Lawyers of America.

Judge LaValle has served in the Military Reserve, and has been active in law enforcement for all of his adult life. He served on the U.S. Customs task force, ran a SWAT patrol, and is licensed as an Arson Investigator. In addition to his law practice, he remains involved on a part-time basis in a successful police agency in what has been called a high-crime area.

LEGACY LAWYER

FOLLOWING IN MY FATHER'S FOOTSTEPS

I have lived, worked and voted in Galveston County, Texas for every one of my 55 years of life. My father was both an attorney and also a politician. He served as state legislator and then as a county judge. I caught on at a very early age that he had prestige, respect, and standing in the community, and I knew that I wanted to do the type of work that he was doing. He was very well known for helping those who needed help or who couldn't stand up for themselves. So, I just aimed myself towards that goal at a very early age.

I had one older brother and two younger sisters, and we had a lot of unique opportunities as children. My father was a personal friend of President Johnson, so we made more than one trip to the White House, and we were certainly there for President Johnson's funeral when I was a young man. Memories like that make for an extraordinary childhood.

While growing up, I was always working. I started working part-time at age 13, and worked all the way through high school, putting myself through college and law school. As a college student, I worked in a chemical plant and was a union member. When I got injured on that job, I understood firsthand the humiliation that one feels when they're not able to report to work and are unable to meet their financial obligations and family obligations. It's something that's kind of carried me through my career.

During my 29 years as an attorney, I've also served as a part-time judge for 12 years; I rose to the rank of Colonel in the military reserve, and I've also worked as a police officer or part-time police officer during all those years. I am the captain of a small police agency in a very crime-ridden area, and we currently have a very active suppression and patrol program that I'm really proud of.

When I became a full-time attorney, I also became a part-time officer, rather like becoming a volunteer firefighter. I have been able to move around quite a bit and have worked in four separate counties. I was on the U.S. Customs task force, and I ran a SWAT patrol. I was actually trying to retire from my position altogether – I've been running the training facility for some time on a part-time basis. Since I hadn't used my brains in law enforcement in a long time, I started taking fire science courses to become an arson investigator, which requires a separate license to a separate state agency. I finally landed a spot as an arson investigator, but it was in a place that had virtually no fires. So, that pushed me back into supervision and management of officers and putting together programs to help them become more effective on the street.

The area is in a very small city surrounded by larger cities such as Houston, Pasadena, and the Port of Houston. Literally, it's possible to step a block outside of the city limits and see people selling drugs or themselves in prostitution. That area is very underserved by the proper jurisdiction, and we do everything possible to keep pushing these people further and further away from the city limits.

Even though I work for a city, state peace officers have a county-wide jurisdiction for felonies, disturbances of the peace, traffic violations, etc. So we do tend to go down roads just outside the city and do patrols. As a slight aside, it seems to me that, regardless of anyone's place on the spectrum of personal politics, parents tend to become cultural conservatives regardless of their past. That's when you start looking at bigger issues that will affect your children and family.

Because I have worked as an attorney, a judge, a police officer and as a soldier, I have a unique perspective on the practice of law and the people on all sides of the law. I've gotten the training and experience to deal with almost any situation that arises. That's probably the most important thing when people are looking for a lawyer, because they need somebody who has a good reputation at the courthouse and with the other attorneys, as well as an attorney with a lot of fight in them who can reach the client's goals. Several years ago, I was blessed to attend the U.S. Marine

Corps Command and Staff College (CSC); it really helped my law practice in terms of mindset and preparation, and making sure you have the necessary toolkit to reach the finish line.

I waited until age 48 to have my first child, so I could focus solely on her. My daughter is seven years old; as sole custodian, I have been raising her on my own for quite some time. She's very tall and independent, and out-negotiates me all the time. When I travel, if I can be away less than 24 hours, I go alone; if I will be away more than 24 hours, she goes with me. Now that she's in first grade, that's going to be a problem, unless I can take her assignments with me.

For years, my daughter had been telling me to go to the hospital and buy a baby because she wanted a little brother. Recently, I was blessed to marry a woman with a five-year-old son who is adoptable, so we're just starting the adoption process now. He was born in the United States but knows Spanish as a second language because of the time he spent in El Salvador. While it didn't work out instantly for my daughter to have a baby brother, it is working out now.

They both go to the same private Catholic school where I went as a child, and I'm now on the school board. Since the teachers were so poorly paid, I tried to come up with a solution to be more competitive with other schools. The teachers weren't getting a discount for their own kids to go to the school, so most of them sent their kids to public school. That caused conflict because the teachers would have to leave the campus to care for their own kids, so we started a program to give them tuition time so that the kids could stay with their parents.

My faith formation had a lot to do with my beliefs and ideals as an adult. It just seems that if you put God first, everything else falls into place.

GROWING A FAMILY PRACTICE

My mom has been gone for 15 years now, and my dad has been gone for six years. Since we were both attorneys, I was lucky enough to have shared an office with him in the same building for a number of years. We had the opportunity to work together, and I think we both learned a little bit from each other. It was hard to compete with him because in 1987, he was charging 1957 prices while I was charging 1987 prices. So, there was a bit of contention at the start.

Nor did we agree on my start in the law. When I graduated law school, my father was really advocating for me a join a big law firm and do personal injury work, but I really wanted to strike out on my own – have my own firm. After 29 years of practice, I have offices in my hometown area and downtown Houston; I've been blessed with the cases that have come in and the quality of the results.

INFLUENCES AND IMPACTS

Before the big Firestone tire recall got a lot of attention, I had a couple of Ford roll-over cases, but nobody in my area was doing them. I knew one lawyer in Arkansas who was handling those cases. When I got my first tire case, I called him because I didn't know anything about tire dynamics. I ended up litigating 246 cases against the Ford and Firestone companies.

The thing that amazed me about this litigation was that the accident reports all read exactly the same as far as the dynamics of the crash - how many times the vehicle rolled, etc. In one accident, the vehicle occupant was ejected, and was dead before coming to rest because they hit an object as they flew out of the vehicle. Other accidents were identical; the person would be ejected and wouldn't even stub their toe. So, you could really see the influence of God at work in the way these people's lives were affected by these tragedies. There was no explanation given by experts as to why one occupant had zero injuries and the next occupant died.

There's also no accounting for people's reactions to their situation. It's most humbling that people with severe losses and injuries (paralysis, death, etc.) end up with a closer relationship with God; they usually spend a great deal of time trying to make you comfortable in dealing with their situation. Claimants with lesser injuries often tend to blame God for their misfortunes and have no appreciation or vesting in the process of trying to make them whole.

Once the tire recall occurred, I started actively advertising for the cases. At the time, there were around 162 printed newspapers in Texas, and maybe 53 in Mississippi for my office in Jackson. A lot of cases really came in from those advertisements. My biggest case was for a lady who was a tetraplegic. She was paralyzed so high in her neck that not only was she unable to move, but also her diaphragm was paralyzed. People with this type of injury, if they live at all, typically only live eight years; this lady has been doing wonderfully for 15 plus years now. When I met her, the situation was looking mighty bleak. I haven't spoken with her for several years, but the last I heard, she actually had an RV that she would take out and about. She got to see her kids graduate high school and college, get married, and have kids of their own.

The true blessing in that case was the fact that she received highly specialized, highly qualified medical care at the scene of the accident. She was traveling between Corpus Christi and San Antonio, Texas on a desolate road; there is nothing out there. Her tire failed, the vehicle rolled, and the accident occurred. It just so happened that, in the traffic headed that way, there were two mobile intensive care unit ambulances traveling from one hospital to another. Without their timely care, she might not have made it at all.

Another influential event would be the 9/11 attacks, in terms of its meaning to our personal sense of freedom and security in the United States. Suddenly, everybody became very patriotic. People that I knew, including attorneys, were calling me for weeks afterward with personal questions: "Hey, you've always had a flag at your house. Where can I go and get a flag?" I think that was a positive that came out of a tragic situation. Sadly, some became a little more intolerant as a society, and that's one of the unfortunate effects.

After the attack at Pearl Harbor, it seems that most of the world thought that the United States would never be attacked at home again. It showed our vulnerability, and perhaps, our arrogance. Our military has not advanced a lot since Pearl Harbor in the sense that most soldiers, sailors, and airmen are off on the weekends. They're in town with their families, which kind of leaves the gates open.

As someone who loves the law, I'm also concerned with our current political discourse when it focuses on deporting an entire group of religious people or locking up an entire group of religious people. That happened with the Japanese in World War II; it took a long time to apologize to them, and I don't think the

United States ever made it right. "Hate politics" has no place in the treatment of human lives…but we're big on it.

PERSONALITY TRAITS AND SUCCESS

I'm one of those people who is genuinely happy, but never satisfied. I always feel like there is something I could have done a little bit differently or better. I could have gone to bed a little bit earlier, or awakened earlier and got to work earlier. There's an OCD component to the successful practice of law, and I think you definitely work harder for yourself than you'd ever work for a firm or another person, because you invariably sacrifice a lot of nights, weekends, and holidays.

That's something that's always bothered me about my child; after school, she's in the office while I'm dealing with clients. To some extent, she is growing up like I did, but I would really rather spend the time with her. I keep hoping to reach a point where I can put down all of this work and just volunteer at her school full-time.

Other attorneys practice with me in my firm, and I've been really blessed in my associations with other attorneys. One in particular had eight post-graduate degrees, and I dearly miss the intellectual discourse that he brought to the table. He also taught me not to worry about everything all the time. Any measure of success is directly proportional to how you treat people who work for you in the office, from the receptionist all the way up to the senior paralegals. As a very young attorney, I learned that you couldn't go into court and be dismissive of the clerks, the bailiff, the reporters, etc. They all work for the judge, and if they get their feelings hurt, the judge will be the first one to know about it.

I'm not sure if this is due to my upbringing or something else completely, but if I'm in the courthouse, I say "yes, sir" or "no, sir" while talking to the county judge or the guy at the shoeshine stand. Every single one of them is due the same amount of respect. The position shouldn't qualify them for any more deference. They are all created in the likeness and image of God.

Galveston County, where my main office is, has three county courts of law, probate court, and five district courts. In Harris County, there are 22 district courts and 15 county courts. In every one of these 'small kingdoms', the judge's personality is reflective of every person who works there on a daily basis. If the judge is hard to deal with, then that same arrogance and rudeness is displayed by everybody who works there. If the judge is very laid-back and easygoing, it seems like everybody is laid-back and easygoing. It's interesting to take the personality dynamics of a particular court and try to make it work in your case. If you can do that, then you will be more successful.

It's not possible to get great results all the time, but it can happen. In one of my all-time favorite cases, I merely served as local counsel during the first round of the Fen-Phen diet drug litigation. One lady felt like she needed to lose a little weight to fit into a certain size of dress for her daughter's upcoming wedding. She went to her doctor, got the Fen-Phen prescription, and she lost the weight. Unfortunately, as a direct result of taking these drugs she developed primary pulmonary hypertension, which means that the only thing that will help you is a lung transplant. This very well-litigated case had some of the best and brightest lawyers on the other side, which is my preference because they make you a better attorney. Eventually, we made her wealthy enough to self-fund a lung transplant procedure. At the end of the day, she was able to get the money and her health, which is a once-in-a-lifetime occurrence. I don't know of any personal injury attorneys anywhere who don't want a healthy, wealthy client!

LOOKING TO THE FUTURE

I'm surprised that technology has not advanced more. At this point, I had thought that I would be sending my robot down to the courthouse to argue a case with the Judge's computer. As a little kid, I would go with my dad to court, or hang around the courthouse when he was the county judge; back in the 1960s, when people got divorced, the divorce decree was a one-page fill-in-the-blank form that covered everything. As we've been able to process more and more words faster and more efficiently, not to mention at a lower cost, it's not unusual to see a 40-page or 50-page divorce decree covering all kinds of issues in Texas that the actual litigants never considered.

For instance, some people have lived in the same city and county their entire lives, so the pages and pages of information on passport restrictions and international abduction may not apply. A lot of these just seem like lawyer-created issues. I don't know that people understand their rights regarding their children any better when they read these documents than they did with the one-page, fill-in-the-blank form. I've also noticed that in family law cases, at least in Texas and California, there is a perception that whoever runs to the courthouse first and brings the most money with them wins.

As a child, I recall going to watch a contested custody divorce trial in the '60s, which was extremely rare. The judge of that court gave the attorneys involved (one of whom worked for my dad) a severe dressing-down for being there on a custody case. He finally told the two litigants, "Look, the reason you two are here today is because you both have crummy lawyers. I'm going to order the two of you to go back into the jury room and come out in five minutes and tell me who gets these kids and what the child support is going to be. If you can't figure it out, I'll take the kids away from both of you."

I don't know whether or not he would have actually taken the kids away from them, because they did reach an agreement. It certainly would be subject to a review on appeal. On the other hand, 50 years later, I don't know that our society has advanced all that much. Now we coerce people by saying, "Well, you have to pay for this attorney who will represent the kids, and you have to pay for this person to inspect and evaluate the homes, and you have to pay this mediator." Instead of coercing them with threats about removing the kids, we coerce them by making them spend their life savings or kid's college fund. Typically, the first one to run out of money is ready to fold, and that's a system that sorely needs revamping. That is something that our state senator is going to have to take on in this state.

Unfortunately, in Texas, conservatism has taken over all of the state government and there's a big push to stop what people see as lawsuit abuse or frivolous lawsuits, etc. I've worked through thousands and thousands of lawsuits. Some of them have worked out really well, and some have gotten dumped, but I never filed one in which I didn't believe in the client or didn't believe in the cause. Clients need an advocate to go down there to represent their position. We've become such a conservative state, and so doctor-friendly, insurance-friendly and big business-friendly, but there just doesn't seem to be a whole lot in our state law right now for the individual consumers and taxpayers.

CLOUDS ON THE LEGAL HORIZON

As an attorney, I'm most concerned with the fact that our society is sealing off the right of individuals to go to the courthouse. This may depend on the person you talk to, but when I was a young attorney, you could either say it was a level playing field if you were on the plaintiff's side of the case, or that it was too plaintiff-oriented if you were on the defense side of the case. It used to be that people had a fair shake. Attorneys could do things with a handshake; you could send over your view of the evidence, and get cases settled.

In the state of Texas, the bizarre turnaround is that a case can include a reckless drunk driver speeding who rear-ends somebody, causing catastrophic injuries, and defense attorneys will stand up and tell this to juries: "Well, folks, accidents happen. That's why they're called accidents." Although this hasn't happened to me, I've seen great attorneys with really good cases get thrown right out of court, even when it's obvious that they're representing an injured person who was injured through no fault of their own.

It would be great to know that when people enter the courthouse, it won't be the worst experience of their lives. You would like for people going through divorce court to leave there thinking, "Well, I may not have gotten everything I wanted, but overall this was a fair process. I was treated with dignity and my children's needs are being met." In injury cases, attorneys want people to be able to tell their story to the jury, because telling that story is part of the healing process.

There are a lot of civil rights cases that seem to be summarily dismissed before the injured party has their day in court. There's been a lot of media attention on police-involved shootings in different cities; some of these cases have settled and some of them have gotten thrown out.

I do a lot of civil rights cases, but a great number of those get thrown out of court very early on. My firm files them in state court, the case gets removed to Federal Court, and the Federal Court determines that it wasn't a violation of the Federal law, even though a case doesn't get removed to Federal Court to begin with unless it meets specific and narrow criteria. That means the case will get kicked back to the state court to resolve the state claims; if all federal causes of action get washed out of court very early on. A lot of lawyers haven't caught on to the importance of starting at state court, so that they can return to a court once the federal judge kicks them around some.

I used to take on a lot more medical malpractice cases. Currently, before the case can be filed, the laws require the attorney to find a doctor who is qualified (or more qualified than the doctor on the opposite side) to swear on an affidavit that this other doctor breached the standard of care in a particular area. Now, this legal change was supposedly enacted because of frivolous lawsuits, with the notion of reducing the cost of the doctor's insurance because they're not defending so many frivolous lawsuits. However, doctors are not paying any less in premiums; they are paying just as much or more than they always did. However, these laws keep a lot of consumers, taxpayers, and individual citizens from having their day in court.

This is evident in the television advertisements that describe different drug cases. All of these ads also run in Texas where, for the most part, the law has changed. People who are hurt by drugs in Texas have no recourse, because our Fifth Circuit Court of

Appeals (which is the Federal Appellate Court with jurisdiction on federal matters in Texas, Louisiana, and Mississippi) has ruled on a doctrine called Federal Preemption. Essentially, if the FDA ever approved the drug, then you can presume that it's safe and the case is out of luck. I used to work through a lot of the medical cases on different medications like Fen-Phen. Now the cases that we seem to be doing are much more centered on certain medical devices: IVC filters, Stryker hip implants, transvaginal mesh, and Zimmer knee replacement products.

In Texas, many personal injury lawyers are moving into business-to-business litigation, so they're representing a business suing another business. For some reason, the appellate courts don't chase those cases away like they do with an injured individual. Trucking cases are probably the biggest segment of personal injury cases right now, taking care of people who have been injured by tractor-trailer operators.

AN 18-WHEELER ACCIDENT

One case earlier this year had a really bizarre set of facts. A young man on his motorcycle was going to his job out on the docks in the area of the chemical plants; it was the same area that I worked in when I was his age. At the very last second in the fog, he saw something in the roadway and struck it with his motorcycle. The thing that was in the roadway was the entire rear wheel set of a tractor-trailer. It was literally four tires, wheels and an axle that had fallen off the back of a tractor-trailer.

The driver of that truck, who had just left his yard less than a mile away, didn't even know when it had fallen off because the brakes weren't hooked up to that axle. If the brakes were hooked up, then the brakes would have locked up with the entire vehicle. This young man lost a leg below the knee, but as a diabetic, he's also required several revision surgeries and several prosthetic devices. We've resolved his case and he's eager to get back to work, and he's doing really well. At the same time, there's no amount of money that would make it worthwhile to lose your leg.

The frustrating part in personal injury work is trying to make people whole, without having the actual ability to get them there. An attorney by the name of Jim Perdue wrote a book that meant a lot to people in my line of work; it's called, 'Who Will Speak for the Victim?' His book verbalizes or memorializes the way that a lot of personal injury lawyers feel about what they do for a living. People come to my office who have been put off by insurance adjusters for over a year - a year and a half, a year and nine months, etc. The reason is that the insurance adjusters know that if they can make it to the two-year mark, the case will end and there's no way to bring a lawsuit after that. For instance, with the kid who lost a leg in the tractor-trailer accident, even though the trucking company representatives knew that the kid was represented by counsel, they sent an adjuster to the hospital. The adjuster told him that if he signed these papers, the company would give him around $25,000 and pay his medical bills. Thankfully, he called me without signing anything. Those people were promptly removed from the hospital.

PROCESSING AN ACCIDENT

I received a message from an old friend and long-time client that her adult son was gravely injured and I was needed at the hospital. I was not sure if I was summoned to provide emotional support or perhaps draft a will or power of attorney. Upon arriving and meeting with this terribly- injured man and his family, I realized the type, size and potential value of any claim asserted against the trucking company and so advised the victim and his family. They immediately put me to work.

First and foremost, is preserving the evidence, both the vehicles and the scene. We fired off a letter (e-mail/fax) to the trucking company advising we would go to court and seek an injunction unless they consented to the total sequestering of everything related to the accident. We received an immediate and positive response from a top-tier defense firm with a reputation for being honorable. This bought us time to build my trial team. I needed the best of the following: legal researchers, paralegals, negotiators, litigators, accident reconstruction specialist, heavy truck maintenance specialist, a federal motor carrier inspector (we found 87 separate federal safety violations), engineers, consulting physicians and surgeons, an economist, life-care planner; almost an endless list of vital team players. This case, while never actually filed at the courthouse, was worked up like a trial case and settled in mere months, thanks to the dedication, collegiality, and diligence of the opposing legal teams. While I cannot go into specifics, to say the client had millions of reasons to be happy is an understatement!

THE OTHER SIDE OF THE COIN

There are a lot of unseemly things that happen in my area of law, and I don't have any problem telling anybody that fact. In 1989, I was a young attorney and also a captain with a local constable's office. There was a major industrial accident, a hydrofluoric spill, and every deputy (including myself) was hospitalized because of this acid spill. I was one of the first ones released, maybe because I was one of the youngest and healthiest or because I had the least amount of exposure. As I went back to the hospital for my co-workers who had become my clients, all kinds of lawyers were moving from room to room and trying to sign people up for representation.

That's the other side of the coin; not only the adjusters but some of the attorneys on my side of the docket are not very ethical. One of those attorneys who lurked around in hospitals was a very well-known, well-regarded, but controversial person. He actually complained to the State Bar of Texas that I was trying to take away one of his clients. He produced a plane ticket trying to show that he was in Chicago on that day. This was amazing, considering I knew the man and saw him in my client's hospital room. Well, that didn't go very well for him, but I understand his position in terms of wanting to do that.

AVOIDING THE PITFALLS

In my profession, a lot of attorneys either burn out early, ruin their physical health, or develop other issues: depression, substance abuse, alcohol abuse, etc. I think that it's due to the overwhelming realization that you're the only best and last choice these people have to try to resolve their issue. I think that attorneys tend to internalize everybody's problem and take it on as our own in order to try and level the playing field and fix that fight. It's a huge burden that some people take on and internalize.

In some situations, I've gotten the client a good result, but they squandered away the money and then came back wanting me to go back to the case and get more money, which unfortunately never happens. I try to recommend annuities and other things, where the money will last a lifetime, or at least a substantial number of years. Of course, all sorts of pirate outfits try to buy the annuities at a discount, and pay the claimant something like

19 to 23 cents on the dollar. When we settle a case on an annuity, the annuity is supposed to be non-revocable.

For example, say that a claimant won a settlement of three million dollars. Rather than give the claimant three million dollars today in a lump sum, depending on the arrangement, they receive a certain amount of money now and then a certain amount of money monthly, quarterly, or annually. The notion is to let the bulk of the money earn some interest and keep the payments going longer because they may have medical needs for a lifetime, and nobody wants them to blow their money on houses or luxuries when they need the money for their healthcare.

Some companies, like J.G. Wentworth, advertise very aggressively; if you won the lottery or you were given a medical annuity, they'll buy it out today. What the company doesn't tell people is that their representative will only pay you about 19 to 39 cents on the dollar for the annuity. These things are not meant to be sold, but people manage to find their way around that rule somehow.

Ironically, now that it's tougher for injured and medical patients to sue their doctors and hospitals, medical mistakes seem to be at an all-time high. While there seems to be less oversight with physicians and surgeons, a higher number of surgeons seem to be entering the operating room impaired on drugs or alcohol.

This has been a growing trend both in my state and nationally. Medical mistakes are becoming more and more prevalent; there's less accountability, mainly because there are fewer lawsuits and even fewer successful lawsuits out of the ones that are filed. If you get into a Ford Explorer today, at least one of those stickers inside that Ford Explorer pertaining to the vehicle flipping over is a direct result of litigation that I've been involved in. So, attorneys do have a function in trying to keep society safe.

JUSTICE AND THE BOTTOM LINE

Probably my worst experience was my very first product liability case. I was a young attorney down in Texas City when a police officer (one that I knew), a few years older than me, called and said his brother was a soldier in Fort Hood, Texas. His brother had some kind of problem at Fort Hood, and he needed me to investigate the situation. When I arrived, the police had arrested the brother and his wife. A CPS representative had taken two kids out of their house, and a baby had died in the house. That was the limit of my information for the first 48 hours.

Since the police and CPS thought that this soldier and his wife had murdered their baby, they had done as you might expect. They removed the kids from the house and filed a murder case on the parents. I did some digging around, and contacted everybody I could think of as a resource who would help explain the situation. In a very short time, I realized that this baby's death was totally accidental and preventable, due to positional asphyxia. This family had a child aged three or four, and they had newborn twins. One of the newborn twins had a cold. So, because one baby had a cold and they didn't want the other baby to get sick, they put the baby in a play-pen and presumed, like any parent would, that the play-pen is a device that's manufactured for the safety of the baby. For instance, if the mom had to mop the kitchen floor or vacuum the living room, she would put the baby in the play-pen to keep the baby enclosed and safe.

Well, the flooring material of the play-pen was a hard surface, and the sides that met the flooring material were mesh. The mesh had stretched out and the baby was crawling around on the floor of the play-pen. He got his head to the edge of it, right at the spot where the mesh was worn and loose. The baby's head, in trying to lay down, just went over the side in this little area and put pressure on the baby's neck. That stopped the blood and oxygen flow. Our firm got the couple released from jail and the kids were returned to them. Then, we started a product liability case against the manufacturer of the play-pen.

I put together some money, and hired some engineers, to try and learn the physics of the thing. In the course of organizing this case, my expert designed a little item that, for eight cents, would retrofit and fix this play-pen. So, we met with the manufacturers, whose lawyers were located in the Saint Paul/Minneapolis area, and said, "Look, regardless of how this litigation goes, we want to give you this item. At the end of the day, you can fix the play-pens that you have on the market. Also, you can take this design and sell it to the other manufacturers to recoup your cost for fixing your products."

The manufacturers rejected the item because, at that time, there were only a few annual reported deaths (around 1.3 on average). Since the company only got sued every few years, in their mind, it was a lot cheaper for a few dead babies along the way than to fix their product. Because of that, I got involved with filing things with the Consumer Product Safety Commission and other regulatory agencies, trying to get these guys to see the error of their ways. As a young lawyer, with no kids of my own, it literally made the hair stand up on the back of my neck, though I tried not to show any emotion as I heard it. It's kind of what they say about playing poker; you're playing the people at the table and not the cards in your hand.

The sad part about these sorts of cases is that these parents could literally have ended up in prison and lost their other children forever. In these few deaths around the country, typically the parents blame themselves and each other, they become alcoholics, they get divorced, etc. That's why nobody was going after the companies. Plus, at the time, if you walked into your lawyer's office, who had handled your divorce, a DWI or your will, and said, "I want to sue this manufacturer in another state," they wouldn't have a clue about how to proceed. So, it would probably sit on the family attorney's desk until the statute of limitations expired. I'm just trying to keep a very open mind and evaluate everything that comes through to figure out if there's a wrong that needs to be righted.

THOUGHTS ON UNUSUAL LEGAL CASES

I have always maintained a general practice but it has moved in different directions over the years. At one time, I was only doing product liability while on the Ford Firestone docket, etc. At other times, I've done like any small town lawyer would do in terms of having a criminal docket and a family docket. One of the most bizarre cases I ever handled was an ex-wife's DWI trial. That was a lot of fun because I got to tell the jury panel, "You've noticed that we have the same last name. As the hours and days wear on, you'll find out why I don't like her but don't hold that against her." I beat up on her just enough that they felt sorry for her, and cut her loose; since the goal was to get her out, that strategy worked for that case.

Many years later, an old girlfriend contacted me who was also charged with a DWI. Although I had quit doing criminal altogether, she had a very interesting situation in that every type of evidence in the world that could be gathered was there against her. I wanted to give this trial a shot. For some reason, the judge of this particular court isn't very well liked by the defense counsel, but I always thought that the judge was very fair and very honorable; he always treated me and my clients really well. Anyway, when we arrived for the trial date, the judge wasn't there. He served on the judicial conduct commission, so on that day, he had to go to the state capital and hear cases in which people would file complaints against judges. So, a visiting judge arrived for our trial; although I wasn't aware of her presiding over criminal cases anywhere, she was a very well-known female civil judge who had also taught at a local law school.

As this trial wore on, any time I stood up, I was just shot down. All of my objections were shot down, my expert (who was more qualified than the prosecution's expert) was disqualified, and it really felt like I was getting beat up during the entire trial. While the jury went out to deliberate on the verdict, I guess the judge felt like she hadn't messed with me enough. As a condition to my client's bond, although my client didn't have bond conditions, the judge added that my client had to take an immediate drug test at the courthouse. Then she ruled that if the drug test showed any alcohol or drugs in my client's system, that she was sending that evidence into the jury room. Since the evidence was already closed off, there was no more evidence to be received. My client's actions on the day of trial had nothing to do with guilt or innocence at the time of the arrest.

Typically in Houston, the 'baby prosecutor' in the courtroom is trying the case while the chief prosecutor is supervising the trial to guard against mistakes. Once the jury goes out, the chief prosecutor goes to the office and leaves the baby prosecutor in the courtroom to await the jury's verdict. Meanwhile, I was objecting by doing something called 'making a bill' on the case, by putting some things into the record to use later if I had to appeal. On the other side, the baby prosecutor absolutely refused to have her boss come back down because she wanted to handle it. Well, the long and the short of the story is that the jury came back with a 'not guilty' verdict before the drug test occurred. The judged ordered that the drug test be done anyway. In essence, my client was held in custody after being found not guilty; she had to pay 11 dollars for a drug test and have somebody watch her urinate. I was told to come back the next morning so that the court could consider the results of the test. I ended up suing the judge, the prosecutor's office, the county, the sheriff, the probation department, everybody I could think of in Federal court. Eventually, the Federal court ruling stated that because the judge still had jurisdiction to sign the dismissal at the end of the case, the judge was immune.

However, the judicial conduct commission handled my client's complaint separately; the judge of the court had to recuse himself from the commission since he had hired the female civil judge for that case. Now she only visits in civil and family cases; she's not allowed to do criminal work anymore. I would have thought that any high school kid who had taken a government or history class would know that you couldn't treat somebody like that, but apparently at least one law school graduate sitting a few feet away from me didn't get that lesson either. The Judge was firmly rebuked by the judicial conduct commission.

THINGS NEW ATTORNEYS SHOULD KEEP IN MIND PHILOSOPHICALLY SPEAKING

Over the years, law firms tend to expand and contract; I've seen them come and go. I've seen attorneys flounder or file for bankruptcy, and lawyers have lost their licenses because of ethical absences. The bottom line is that the legal profession is really a business. You should want to do some pro-bono work and other things for the community, but you have to reach a point of realization that your time and resources are limited, so you can't help everybody who comes in needing help. So, you have to pick and choose your cases, and take on a few that you feel will guarantee you success; after that, you will have the luxury of having more time available, and more money to donate to causes. Literally, I would have gone out of business 25 years ago if I had taken on every hard-luck story just because the people needed help. There's a very fine line of running the business and running the law firm.

I consider myself moderately successful. There was a story on national news about a local attorney, Joe Jamail, who just died at the age of 90 with a net worth of $1.7 billion. He was working on the Pennzoil Texaco case with a billion-dollar fee as I was just starting out as a lawyer. Certainly there are more successful lawyers in the world, but I've also met a lot of brilliant attorneys who really seem to lose their way in their success. In a room with two attorneys as co-counsel on a case, I listened to them argue over who owned the better jet. There just wasn't enough space in the room for all three of our egos, so I left the room.

Texas is one of those states that have board certifications, which means that you can get recognized as a specialist in one of many areas of law. I've never felt the need to get a board certification, and a few of the smartest and most successful lawyers I knew never pursued that. I was invited into some fellowships and professional societies along the way that really meant a lot to me. When I settled my first case for over a million dollars, I was invited to join the 'Million-Dollar Advocates Forum', which is a group of trial lawyers who have been able to get a million-dollar settlement or verdict for their client; the Forum represents less than one percent of attorneys everywhere. Years later, I was asked to join the Multi-Million Dollar Advocate Forum for lawyers who have settled cases at two million dollars and higher, which is a little bit rarer.

Somehow I got an excellent rating from Avvo.com, which is a website that shows ratings for doctors, lawyers, and dentists. The accolades that make me really proud are from the American Academy of Trial Attorneys (another lawyer nominated me for membership), and Rue's Ratings, which is supposed to pick out the 100 best attorneys in every state. This is a great honor since the state of Texas has something like 93,000 attorneys. I am not sure about their criteria, but I'm hoping that it has something to do with what I'm trying to teach my two children: do the right thing for the right reason.

In my first time at Federal Court, I was clueless about when to stand up or speak. Without really strong mentoring, there will definitely be some fumbling along the way, but it's best to keep arrogance out of it, and just say, "This is my first time doing this." Attorneys are not quite as collegial in our profession as we used to be, but plenty of people will step up to help. I can recall being at hearings far from home, while the day became night faster than anticipated, and needing to get back for a childcare issue. Attorneys who did not know me just stepped up and asked if they could finish whatever task I was doing so I could get on the road. There's still this collegiality, but we have to take ownership of what we do; if we don't know what we're doing, then we just need to let people know, "I need a little help with this."

When I went to law school, they would teach you the information in the books and then turn you loose to figure it out at the courthouse, but there seems to be much better advocacy and mentoring programs now that try to get attorneys ready for that first trial.

New attorneys should keep in mind that they are also a defense to bullying. Just like police officers or a judge, or even the armed forces, attorneys are there to stand up for people who don't have a voice. Soldiers go ahead and dig wells, give medical shots, and feed people. People tend to just think about soldiers in combat operations, but that's a very small part of the armed service job. It's really about going after the world's bullies.

I am an attorney and am damned proud of my profession and its impact on society!

(This content should be used for informational purposes only. It does not create an attorney-client relationship with any reader and should not be construed as legal advice. If you need legal advice, please contact an attorney in your community who can assess the specifics of your situation.)

2

UNDERDOGS AND ADVOCATES: A JOURNEY OF EMPATHY

by Laurie A. Mack-Wagner, Esq.

Laurie A. Mack-Wagner, Esq.
Mack & Santana Law Offices, PC
Minneapolis, Minnesota
www.macksantanalaw.com

Counselor Laurie Mack-Wagner graduated with Highest Honors in the top 5% of her class from Florida State University's College of Law in 1994. She is one of the founding shareholders of Mack & Santana Law Offices, P.C., and has been practicing since 1994 in complex litigation primarily in family law and related causes of action.

Ms. Mack-Wagner has been named a Minnesota Super Lawyer for five consecutive years (2011-2015) and also named on the Top 50 Women Super Lawyers List for Minnesota for three consecutive years (2013-2015), She focuses on developing creative and practical solutions for clients seeking assistance in family law matters and divorce cases.

With her practice based primarily in the Twin Cities area, Laurie frequently teaches at legal education seminars in Minnesota, and is the author or co-author of published articles nationally and statewide. Most notably, Laurie is the co-author of the child support chapter in the Family Law Financial Deskbook, first edition, 2008, plus all the subsequent updates, from Minnesota CLE, and in addition, is the author of the Enforcement and Contempt chapter in the Minnesota Divorce Practice Deskbook, also from Minnesota CLE, new in 2015.

UNDERDOGS AND ADVOCATES: A JOURNEY OF EMPATHY

MY EARLY LIFE

I grew up in Brunswick, Ohio, about 20 miles south of Cleveland. My parents were young sweethearts who met when they were teenagers and are still together after 47 years of marriage. My father spent his whole career as an accountant, while my mother worked as a nurse when she was not a stay-at-home mom. I am the oldest of four kids, with two sisters who are two years and six years younger than I, and a brother who is 11 years younger. My siblings and I have always been close, and I am fortunate to live within 35 miles from all of them.

As a young child, my ambition and curiosity were frequently on display. My parents said that I was a high-energy kid who was always doing something, whether it was making an amusement park out of the backyard or creating artwork to sell. I showed my entrepreneurial spirit when I announced to my father at age five that I would one day be the president of my own company.

My parents were extremely hard-working people themselves, and they instilled in me the attitude that anything is possible through hard work and dedication. My mother was instrumental in helping me develop an affinity for education. She played "school" with me before I was actually going to school, as well as during the summers in my early elementary school years. My parents are highly witty and intelligent people who raised me to think that way. I never had any sense that I was limited to traditional female roles, even though I had a stay-at-home mom at the time.

Brunswick was a typical middle class suburb. Our neighborhood had a community pool and park that was the centralized hangout for the 200 or so houses in the neighborhood. When we were not in school, we spent our time with the neighborhood kids riding bikes and swimming. I joined the neighborhood swim team and excelled at swimming.

It was during my school years in Brunswick that I began an interesting journey that helped to shape who I am today and led to my decision to be a lawyer who advocates for others. My parents thought that a Catholic education would be the best for my sisters and me. However, due to the overcrowding of Brunswick's regular Catholic church, our neighborhood was sectioned off and we were forced to attend a new church that did not have a school in Brunswick. St. Charles well outside of Brunswick in the city of Parma was the school that would allow children from the new church in Brunswick. From grades 5-8, we rode 45 minutes from St. Charles. On the bus with my sister(s) and me were kids from various Catholic schools, some of whom were older and bullied us quite frequently. It was often not a very pleasant ride, but I gained a lot of toughness by learning to stand up for myself and others.

In terms of the quality of education at St. Charles, I would say that it was above average in the traditional sense. All of the core content classes (math, English, social studies and sciences) were thoroughly covered, but elective classes were generally not emphasized. I was eager to learn Spanish, and I finally got the opportunity when I graduated from St. Charles after 8th grade to attend Brunswick High School. It was a difficult adjustment suddenly having 600 students in my class and hardly knowing any of them. But I really appreciated the fact that I could finally take Spanish class. I immediately loved speaking Spanish and learning as much as I could about the Latin American culture. In the process of learning Spanish I decided that I would one day live in Florida because it was warm and I thought I might have an opportunity to use Spanish there in my career, whatever that would be.

When I was 15 years old, I learned that a major change was in store for our family. My dad decided that we needed to move out of state because the accounting profession was not thriving in Ohio. I had dreams of moving somewhere tropical, but we instead discovered that we were headed northwest to Minnesota, a state famous for its freezing temperatures. From a career standpoint, it was an essential move for my dad, as he obtained a corporate controller position for Hutchinson Technology, Inc. (HTI) a budding company in Hutchinson, Minn., that manu-factured computer parts. Emotionally, though, it was quite a shock for all of us, considering that almost all of my mom and dad's entire family lived in Ohio. We were accustomed to large extended family gatherings, and we were headed several states away to live where we knew no one. I had just spent my freshman year getting to know my classmates at Brunswick High, and I was going to be the "new kid" again. In the summer of 1984, my family and I were bound for Hutchinson, Minnesota.

If Brunswick was a typical suburb, Hutchinson could be described as a typical small town. Located 60 miles west of Minneapolis, Hutchinson had a population of about 10,000 at that time, making it less than one-third the size of Brunswick. Although quite small, it was the "big city" for several smaller towns around it. In fact, there was no city as large as Hutchinson within 50 miles. Hutchinson was a rural community with a quaint downtown and a river running through the middle of it. As is common in small towns, the people there were close-knit and all seemed to know each other. They were generally friendly, but it wasn't exactly easy to break into their circle.

At times I enjoyed the attention of being the new kid at Hutchinson High School, but often I longed for a feeling of familiarity. My classmates had all grown up together, while I was an outsider trying to make friends. Hutchinson High did give me a great education though, and it was clear that I excelled in school. I maintained the serious effort toward my classes that I had in Ohio and continued to enjoy learning and challenging myself academically. When I wasn't studying, I was usually working. I got my first job at Hardee's, a fast food restaurant, and then later I worked as a cashier at Shopko (a store similar to Target). I kept the same work ethic at these jobs that I did in the classroom, even though they could be quite mundane. My parents took us on wonderful family vacations. When I was in high school, we traveled to Acapulco, Mexico, which added to my interest in Spanish. It was around this time, when I was 16, that I had my first serious boyfriend. He was a talented football player and good student who lived on a farm south of town. I liked him so much that I eventually married him.

By the age of 18, I made the somewhat surprising decision to become a lawyer. It was an interesting decision not because law itself is a unique field, but rather because I had no lawyers among my family, friends, or even acquaintances. I had no "attorney role model." I was going to pave a completely new path for myself.

I chose to attend Mankato State University in Mankato, Minnesota, which was about 65 miles from Hutchinson. Mankato State was a good fit for me because it was a reputable state school and much more affordable than the private schools I was interested in. Another key factor was that my boyfriend, who was a year older than I, was already going there.

In the summers, I kept busy working in Hutchinson. My main gig was doing production work at HTI where my father worked. My dad called this a "character building" job because it was grueling shift work examining parts for eight hours each day using a microscope or putting sheets of metal into a developer and catching them at the end. I worked either second or the third ("graveyard") shift but I was glad to have the job. My more enjoyable, part-time job involved custom framing at a local art gallery and store. For extra money in the summer, I tutored college statistics, and while at Mankato I worked in the university's computer science department as an assistant secretary. I sold fruit baskets during the breaks. To say that I kept busy with work and school would be an understatement.

I originally went to Mankato on a computer science scholarship but soon decided I was bored with it. Weighing my options, I knew that I needed to have a good backup degree in case I decided to get married and to work instead of pursuing law school. I arrived at business administration with a concentration in marketing, and threw in Spanish as a second major just for fun. During my sophomore year, my boyfriend and I studied abroad at the University of Guadalajara and the Centro De Idiomas in Mazatlan as part of MSU's "Winter in Mexico" program. Our group lived with various families, and we attended school for a few hours each day. It was an incredible experience that felt like a four-month vacation, and I realized how much more to life there was outside of Minnesota. My semester in Mexico also taught me to enjoy the moment and not think too much about what is next.

In the summer between my junior and senior year of college I married my high school sweetheart. We were completely broke, but qualified for college aid which allowed us to live in government-subsidized housing while we continued our college courses and worked. I was starting to think since I was married so young that I may get a full-time job right after school, forgo law school, and eventually start raising a family which at that time was what my mom wanted for me. My burning desire to practice law was too strong, however, and I knew I wouldn't be content without making it happen. When I was on the fence about this decision my dad told me that I would have many years of working, day in and day out, and I should pick the career I truly wanted and not settle. Three more years of law school in the grand scheme of life was insignificant. What he said made total sense to me, and I was back on track.

LAW SCHOOL YEARS

I stayed close to Hutchinson to obtain my degree at MSU, but I was eager to go somewhere much warmer for law school. I couldn't handle the brutal Minnesota winters anymore, and my strands of hair turned into icicles as I walked outside after swimming at the college. It was definitely time for a change. Fortunately, I was accepted at Florida State University College of Law. I was ecstatic to be heading to sunny Florida, but unexpectedly I had to stay in Minnesota the summer before law school and all the preferred summer jobs were gone. In order to raise the funds to move I had to work at McDonald's in Hutchinson during the summer. I had just graduated #1 out of 3,908 students with a degree in business and Spanish. This was certainly another "character building" experience but I accepted it as a necessary means to an end. I was always careful to never be too "proud" for a job for which I was overqualified. It was a still a job that I took seriously, and it helped me get where I needed to be. With the funding in hand and a U-Haul behind us, my husband and I took the 1,400 mile trek southeast to Tallahassee, Florida.

I had been an exceptional student during high school and college, but when I took the LSAT (Law School Admission Test), my score was above average but not what I had hoped. People told me that the LSAT was the measuring stick to which the school paid the most attention, but I didn't accept that. I wasn't going to be held to any sort of "average" standard so I worked hard and studied for 2 weeks straight before the one sole test for each class. I tried to join study groups but quickly learned that people in those groups were confusing me more than helping me and the whole process seemed inefficient. It was better for me to study in my solitary, traditional way at my low budget, cockroach friendly apartment across the street. For the weeks leading up to the finals (the sole grade for almost every law school class) I read the books, drafted outlines, and put in the grueling hours at the kitchen table. Despite not enjoying study groups, I enjoyed law school and meeting people like me – passionate about the law and arguing points. My efforts paid off. At one point during my first year at FSU, I was number one in my class and I was invited to the Law Review. The Law Review helped me tremendously in law school. I would advise any student to do whatever it takes to qualify for Law Review because it definitely helps with job placement after graduation.

Law school was an interesting experience for me. Many people in law school are highly competitive people who have a tradition of lawyers in their family. These students came from generations of lawyers from FSU, a school heavily supported by alumni. I was a girl from Minnesota who didn't have any lawyers in her family tree. I was accustomed to the role of "underdog," however, and it only served to motivate me even more. I enjoyed the fact that I was going to make it on my own.

Meanwhile, my husband and I had been growing apart. We divorced right after I finished law school. When I was at FSU, I frequently flew back and forth to visit my family in Minnesota. On one of my visits, I informed my family that I wanted to live in Florida permanently. They were a little bummed out given the closeness of our family, but they were completely supportive and probably not surprised given my disdain for cold climates. At the time, they thought I would never live in Minnesota again. Neither did I.

BEGINNING MY LEGAL CAREER

After my first year of law school, I was hired by a large firm as a law clerk. My legal writing teacher recommended me and it was an important step for getting my foot in the door with a big law firm. My career continued to improve during that time. During the summers and the school year, I continued to work for Carlton Fields (it has since merged to form Carlton Fields Jorden Burt, LLP), a large law firm in Florida that employed about 190 people back then. Most of the employees worked at the Tampa location. I was brought to Tampa as a summer associate after my second year, which is a much better position than law clerk. I faced stiff competition from students from Ivy League schools like Harvard and Yale, but Carlton Fields eventually awarded me one of the positions. Even so, I still had to prove myself for the firm to hire me full-time as a lawyer, which it did at the end of the summer before my last year.

After graduating from FSU, I was off to Carlton Fields to work in their main Tampa office. I began in corporate complex litigation and employment law, which means I was in two different departments. I felt grateful and excited for the opportunity with Carlton Fields, but I was also somewhat lonely. I was recently divorced and until that point had never been alone in my life. I was always able to handle being the outsider at various points in my life, but I previously always had someone close in my corner with me to help me deal with ups and downs I experienced. When I moved to Tampa it was just me – no family and no friends – to fend for myself in a city I knew nothing about.

I came to realize that I liked employment law but I didn't care much for corporate complex litigation, even though I excelled in that area. I knew I was going to be pulled in that direction because I excelled, but in my heart it was not want I wanted to do. As I spent more and more time in Miami, AJ Barranco, Jr., an attorney who handled multi-millionaire divorces, recruited me. He made me an offer that I couldn't refuse. After working and competing for years to get the job with Carlton Fields, practically overnight I decided to leave it at all behind and moved to Miami into an office focused on mainly high-end divorces, although there was some complex civil litigation.

One of the reasons that I left a very secure position to do something so risky – and in a field of law that I didn't know at the time - was to grow as a litigator in an edgier environment and one that I thought had a better potential to reward individual achievement. Partly, I was bored with the corporate complex litigation work at Carlton Fields and knew there was no escaping it there. Family law sounded far more intriguing. In law school, I thought that family law would be the absolute worst thing to do. The majority of people in my class felt the same, and family law was generally viewed as a practice area for those who couldn't rise to the top of the profession. In other words, lawyers practiced family law because it was their only option, not because they wanted to do so. Furthermore, many large firms stay as far away from family law as possible. Obviously, my opinion of family law changed drastically after law school. It may have been unpopular among many colleagues and a bit of a gamble for me, but I had discovered a passion for family law and I had to follow it.

I loved Miami immediately. It was fast-paced, exciting and had a strong Latin American culture. Working for AJ at his small boutique law firm was a total contrast from the experience I had working for a large firm, but AJ taught me a lot about how to be an excellent trial lawyer. The background and training that I received as an associate with Carlton Fields was the quieter, more sophisticated side of law, and the training was organized and structured. Attorneys at Carlton Fields were generally amiable, thorough, and took a more civilized approached to litigation. AJ, on the other hand, is like a "cowboy" from the

Wild West. He is excellent at what he does, but he was nothing like the lawyers I was accustomed to working with before. It was beneficial to observe so many lawyers whose approaches were polar opposites then adopt what I liked most from each of them. I have to say that AJ gave me the most practical tips when it came to practicing law, running a practice, and developing my career to this day. The lawyers at Carlton Fields were undoubtedly excellent at their jobs, but as baby lawyer I simply was not privy to the management aspects of running a practice given the number and depth of lawyers.

I had a friend from law school who was working with an associate of AJ's and he asked me to form a partnership with him. We made the leap together with AJ's blessing. AJ sent us smaller cases to help us get started. We set up a firm and we did really well until my friend and I finally had a falling-out. Luckily, AJ welcomed me back with open arms.

In 1998, I flew back to Minnesota for my brother's high school graduation. While I was out in Hutchinson, I met a man who would become my second husband. He flew back and forth between the Twin Cities and Miami for a while but eventually moved to Miami to live with me. I was doing very well and had my entire career in Florida, but my husband was miserable. He was a die-hard Minnesotan suddenly transplanted to Miami, and he missed home terribly. He badgered me every day until I agreed to move back to Minnesota.

My parents, who were convinced I would never move back home, will be forever grateful to him for bringing me back home to them. We also wanted to have kids, and we both thought Miami was a much more difficult place to raise a family than the Twin Cities. As we assessed it, we realized that both of our families –

both his and mine – were in Minnesota so it made sense for us to go there. In retrospect, and from a purely business perspective, it was quite a sacrifice for me. I was doing well in Miami as a young family law attorney and building up a successful professsional network. I didn't know any employers in Minnesota or even any lawyers in Minnesota, and I had no license to practice law in Minnesota. But love will make us all do crazy things, so I did the unthinkable and returned to the tundra of Minnesota. Thankfully I was able to waive into Minnesota.

At the age of 30, I was getting the itch to settle down and raise a family of my own. My husband and I looked closely at the Twin Cities area because of the promising job prospects it offered. We were ready for a fresh start once again, optimistic that we could design our lives however we wanted.

MY MOVE BACK TO MINNESOTA

We were able to get a place with lake access near Prior Lake, which is a decent-sized lake about 30 miles south of Minneapolis. We purchased a boat and enjoyed regularly going on the water. I had no trouble finding employment either. I was hired by a small firm that did very sophisticated and complex family law cases, which was right up my alley. Through my cases there I met other older professionals (opposing counsel) who did similar work and became valuable mentors to me. I also made a point to participate in the important networking events for family law attorneys.

After a while, while working for the small boutique firm, I realized I wasn't born to be "number two" and I felt I either had to move up in the firm or leave. I had learned what I needed to about Minnesota law and I had made connections by then. I was determined to make some changes. Also, I had just had my daughter, Haley. During the pregnancy I'd developed a terrible condition called Hyperemesis Gravidarum (HG), which results in severe nausea, vomiting, weight loss and dehydration. I had to be on IVs most of the time to keep me alive because I couldn't keep food or water down. My battle with HG was a significant distraction and made me feel like I was sucked away from my career. I had to claw my way back from it because I was in the hospital during much of my pregnancy. Since there is a high chance of HG reoccurring with subsequent pregnancies, I didn't have another child of my own. All the suffering was worth it however, because I have a wonderful 14-year old daughter.

OPENING MY OWN LAW FIRM

One of the things that AJ always said to me was "You're the only person who's really responsible for your career. You have to make the decisions about it, and you can't expect somebody else to do it for you." I assessed my situation at the small firm in Minnesota and I didn't see it as allowing to put myself out there enough as a trial attorney. On top of that, I wasn't getting along with my husband at all and my marriage seemed to be failing. It was time for a change. I decided I was going to leave the firm to start my own practice. I did not have enough savings for six months' living expenses, the recommended amount when starting a new business, but I took the risk anyway. I was certainly taking a leap of faith. A part of me was scared, but I was excited for the opportunity and challenge of going on my own once again.

In 2004, when Haley was just about three years old, I told my friend and co-worker, Lymari Santana, I was leaving. (My family took the news of the second divorce better than the first one since the idea of divorce was no longer shocking to them due to my first divorce and other such experiences with my siblings.) Lymari, and I are both the same age, we have a very similar work style, and we're really good friends. We both came from out-of-state to work for the same law firm at the same time. Lymari was a JAG (Judge Advocate General's Corps) in the Army; she was and is a very thorough, very excellent lawyer. I told her I was leaving and she said, "I'm coming with you." With that, our partnership was born. At first, the firm was called Mack Schaefer & Santana Law Offices, P.C. After my divorce the following year, "Schaefer" was chopped off and the firm was renamed Mack & Santana Law Offices, P.C., the name we have kept ever since. Lymari and I gave considerable thought to marketing right from before we even opened our doors. One of my majors in college was marketing, and I knew the importance of a solid marketing plan. With lawyers all around us, we needed to stand out and emphasize what made us unique. We thought critically about a number of key factors, including our target market, the location, and the type of lawyers we wanted to be. We made our plans, put our procedures in place, and executed them. It has been an amazing experience that both of us have grown tremendously from. When we started the firm, we had a number of challenges. We were used to living fairly comfortably, but during the inception of the firm it wasn't easy to make ends meet. Lymari borrowed money and I had to use my credit cards to pay living expenses. We also decided from the start that we needed to em-ploy a paralegal to assist us in order to be efficient for our clients. While necessary, it was a big financial commitment to pay a para-legal salary given we were living on borrowed funds ourselves. Despite these early financial hardships, neither Lymari nor I have regretted starting our own firm and leaving stable employment.

Lymari and I work hard to make sure that we have covered all of our marketing avenues, make ourselves visible, and remind our clients that we're still around. The number one thing that we consistently strive for is a commitment to excellence; however, it is not about marketing per se, but doing excellent work. Our clients are coming to us in times of personal crisis and are counting on us to do whatever we can to improve their situation. It's a major responsibility, and we don't take it lightly. We get most of our business through referrals now because our clients and other lawyers are familiar with the quality of our work.

Lymari and I co-wrote a chapter on child support for the Minnesota Family Law Financial Desk Book, which was published in 2008, and we've done updates since then. In this last edition, we merged with other advanced child support people, so four of us have co-written our chapter together. This last year in 2015, Lymari and I both wrote one chapter each for a divorce practice manual through the Minnesota CLE (Minnesota Divorce Practice Desk book). We speak and teach, and I do a lot of charity work mainly through the Prior Lake Rotary Club.

Both of us really love the action and excitement of downtown Minneapolis. When Lymari and I decided what kind of lawyers to be we said, "We want to be downtown lawyers." As we were in this beautiful skyscraper, we decided that instead of going out in the suburbs, buying a small building and creating equity in the small building, we would pay rent but be happy and in the middle of the action. This model works for us.

In our off time, we both live in lake homes; she lives in Plymouth on Medicine Lake. We both appreciate the fact that these offer us a respite from the chaos of the big city. It's the best of both worlds.

THE BLEND — FAMILY LIFE NOW

Moving back to the personal side, I was divorced from my second husband for quite a few years while still living in my neighborhood in Prior Lake. My daughter was having play dates with a little five-year-old at that time and her dad had recently become single. We had been trading our children back and forth for a while when he eventually asked me out. We got married shortly thereafter and he has been my husband for seven and a half wonderful years now. I learned to golf starting on our first anniversary, and it has been a huge part of my life ever since. The most amazing part of golf is that I originally started learning it for my husband. I thought, "He likes golf and we just got married. He's never going to be happy leaving his new wife at home for five hours at a time." Now, I'm absolutely an addict. Even though I'm not especially good at golf, I always like a challenge. I'm always in competition with myself, and I'm gradually improving my game.

We had some luck with our blended family, and I'm very grateful for the family that we have. I have primary custody of Haley and he has primary custody of his two kids, Autumn and Colton, so the girls actually managed to live that crazy dream of their best friend becoming their sister. They've been raised like twins this whole time. All through elementary school they were in the same class, and the teacher always recommended that they be together. Now they're in the same middle school and they both turned 14 two days apart. Colton is 12 years old. I am often reviewing with him all of the different video games he likes and the games that are his favorites and why. It's very interesting having this experience with a young man. I consider myself to be blessed because I always wanted to have three kids. After my awful pregnancy, it was clear I wasn't going to be able to have them myself, so I ended up getting them in a different way. We're super happy with our blended family, and I think that's because of my colorful life experience, I can actually relate to my clients who are undergoing a life-changing family law event.

Every other weekend, I have this cool experience of having totally selfish "me time" with my husband while the kids go do things with the other parents. Of course we want to have our kids all of the time, but we decided to make the most of the situation. My husband and I get 48 hours to do things like golf non-stop or do some other hobby. This has all led to a greater work/personal life balance and I really love it. Like I said, I'm not very good at golf and I didn't learn from my husband initially. I learned from a group class and then I worked with a pro who helped my husband on an advanced level. Now we both get to touch up with pro lessons. My husband was smart in his approach when he introduced me to the game; he sold me on the appeal of all the outfits. Amazingly, I found that golf has many sound business benefits because it's a wonderful way to meet people in my profession. There are always different charity events and tournaments in which I can participate. There aren't too many women who like to play (compared to men), and I've been able to make a lot of good friends, connections, and referrals this way. It has been a really good marketing avenue, which surprised me.

I've taken many chances along the way and there have been failures. I've not always succeeded at everything, especially in the marriage department. I wouldn't call two divorces "success" but we take chances and we live and learn through it all.

INFLUENCES ON MY LIFE

My family has been a great influence in my success. They always liked my fiery spirit and reinforced the idea that there were no limits on accomplishment. My dad reminded me that as I predicted, I am now the president of Mack & Santana Law Offices, P.C. My dad works for me as my office administrator two days a week now that he has retired from his former employment. Since my parents had me when they were very young, their ideas and attitude are pretty progressive and forward-thinking. It never occurred to them that because I was a girl that doors might be closed to me. I was always sure that I had access to anybody and anything that I wanted.

My experience at St. Charles Catholic School also had a tremendous impact on my success because it made me mentally tough. As I discussed in my opening, when the school in our town was full and no longer able to take students, I was transported by bus to 45 minutes away to St. Charles. The bus ride was a nightmare because of the bullies on the bus. The school was dreary, and the nuns were mean. I felt like a total outsider. It was terrible, but I did not wallow and feel sorry for myself. Since I was the oldest among the children, I had to defend the younger kids from our school on the bus against the bullies who terrorized us. I found myself in numerous fistfights, and I was beaten up plenty of times. But I became much stronger from it. Any time that you have to work your way through a problem and face your fears, it builds your character. I wouldn't want to repeat that time but it was a good thing for me in the end.

I faced another difficult adjustment my family moved from Ohio to Minnesota. Getting used to Hutchinson was really hard and served to toughen me up even more because I wasn't really accepted there. I didn't feel like I really fit in until law school because there were fiery people like me at FSU who were interested in the same things that interested me. Suddenly, I wasn't the only one who wanted to know why things turn out the way they do and what happens in the evolution of the law. I finally felt included again. This profession continues to connect me with people who have that type of personality, and to this day at parties it is not uncommon for the family law attorneys to be excited talking about the law. My point is that the experience of sending me to school 45 minutes from home and moving me across the country wasn't the best and it made me miserable at the time. I now know that I'm a stronger person because of it. I suppose that my parents helped me in that way as well.

Another major influence was my introduction to the business world at a young age. In Brunswick, I lived in a neighborhood where we all knew each other. I wanted money so my dad suggested that I start a babysitting business. I created and delivered around 200 flyers in my neighborhood. In a short time, I had this thriving babysitting enterprise. My dad mass-produced my flyers at work and then I went door-to-door to deliver them. When I got clients, I had to keep all of that organized on a calendar. I may not have opened my law firm until I was 35, but I became an entrepreneur at age 11. I didn't stop there, however. I had a paper route. (Once, I delivered catalogs for a company that paid ten-cents per catalog.)

Those were good lessons. When you are organized, do great work, and you advertise yourself, you can make money. You have to make yourself available and have appointments scheduled properly; however, if you stay organized and are on top of the work, you can succeed. My first experience in business for myself helped me to learn those lessons, and I came away feeling capable. The fact that I was a scrapper who enjoyed fighting for the underdog and the fact that I enjoyed building my own successful enterprises have all added to my skillset. They made the field of law a natural choice for me even though there were no lawyers in my family. My determination to get a business degree has helped me in a big way. It's a perfect partnership with my law degree as running a firm successfully does not only depend on practicing law well. There are all those administrative functions that I see many solo or small firm lawyers struggling to manage. My business degree was also a natural fit for family law, as our firm handles many divorces involving one or both of the parties owning an interest in a closely held business.

ADULT TURNING POINTS

My training is the event that influenced my life as an adult. As I mentioned before, I had a super-secure job that I had to fight aggressively for four years to obtain and I just ditched it overnight because I was concerned about being bored and sheltered. I decided that it would be much more exciting to work with someone who did the kind of cases that AJ did.

On my first day at work, I arrived late, thanks to my friend who also worked as an attorney there and who was driving us to work. I walked into AJ's incredible offices that looked like they were out of the pages of *Architectural Digest* upset that I was running late because of my friend. AJ came in and said, "When I tell you 8:30, I don't mean 8:32, got it?" That was the "hello" I received on my first day of work. I was shocked. I had heard stories about the high turnover given AJ's demanding nature. I thought, "How am I going to survive here? I cried after my first day because I was worried that I made a bad decision in that my desire for excitement caused me to leave the stable career with Carlton Fields.

That changed when he developed a little respect for me and for my experience which I had to earn. If he would take a path that

I questioned, I would say so and why. I could tell that he was the type who wanted me to provide other ideas and opinions and not just blindly do what he said.

AJ taught me a lot. He would give me a project and say, "Okay, I want you to research this and let me know what you find out." The first time, I researched all the options thoroughly and then gave him a list of options. Later, he came into my office and told me, "I didn't hire you just to tell me all my options so that I'd have to make the decision alone. I want you to take a chance and pick one." He then told me that he knew that he expected me at times to be dead wrong, and he would then disagree with me, but he explained that it was only through sticking my neck out that I would be a leader and not a follower.

AJ was right. While you grow as a lawyer, you need to learn to make the call. Sometimes there's no right answer so you just make a decision with your judgment and your instincts. If you start making those calls while you're learning, you get better and better at it. You begin to develop confidence about what to do in each instance and why. That doesn't mean that you need to be overly confident. It's better to tell the client that there's no case law on this particular point but based on these three options, I'm recommending the third approach, for example. On the other hand, you can explain that there are no real guidelines and the outcome really depends upon the judge. In this instance, you need to analyze the factors that come into play and state what you believe the best course of action is to achieve the desired result. Learning to take chances and make tough decisions will help you to become a very confident lawyer. You eventually become comfortable in your skin as a lawyer. Getting to that point really helped me and I think it shaped me into who I am today. I took a crazy chance by giving up a solid job to go work with AJ, and it turned out to be one of the best career decisions I have made.

For all of the stages of growth I went through at a professional level, failing at marriage was a huge period of personal growth for me. It was very hard but it was a very positive lesson that made me realize I don't have it all figured it out. I make mistakes like everybody else. In my line of work, this realization helps you relate to what people are going through. I had no clue as to what it was like to be single and alone until I actually went through it myself.

Having a child is the greatest accomplishment of my life. As a single mom who was also a busy professional, I realized how tough I could be when I had to be tough. It taught me how to stay up all night with a child who has pink eye and then conduct a trial the next day. It's pretty liberating to know that you can juggle priorities and do it very well while thinking on your feet in the process.

PHILOSOPHICALLY SPEAKING

I think I've created my own lifestyle. Being who I am is part of my philosophy on success and definitely working hard is part of the correct combination. You have to be thorough and do a good job. I tell my kids exactly what my dad and my mom told me, "Don't do anything halfway." If you're going to do something, then do it right. The reputation of our firm is that we're really thorough and our work quality is like that of a large law firm with lots of associates. Doing things right is part of my background and it's part of Lymari's background as well. She excelled in the JAG Corps, so she too is very thorough and our work reflects that.

It helps to play to your strengths. For instance, I always knew I was going to be a litigator because my strength was arguing. I took speech classes to overcome a little bit of shyness because I knew that I wanted to argue cases in court. Many lawyers do transactional work because their personalities don't fit with being under that kind of pressure. They still negotiate and argue but they do it outside of the courtroom. If I were advising a young lawyer, I'd have to tell him or her of the importance doing your best work always and the importance of paying attention to marketing. This includes keeping in touch with your own clients and reminding them that you're available and still in business.

COMMUNITY INVOLVEMENT AND SUCCESS

I met a lawyer who asked me to join the Prior Lake Rotary. After I went to the meeting and saw the program and general idea, I decided to join and give it two years, even though I was not a big charity-oriented person. When I worked with the large law firm, as part of our billable hour requirements, we performed charity work such as working with Habitat for Humanity. We were required each year to have 200 hours of "quality non-billable" time. With the large law firm, I ran a race, built a house, did pro bono work, and worked as a lawyer for a guardian. AJ was less structured with quality non-billable work, but he operated in many areas socially and professionally.

More recently, when I was asked to join the Rotary, I didn't really know very many people in my own community but my kids were getting older and I wanted them to realize that they should give back to others whenever possible. After I started attending, I found I truly enjoyed it. One of my activities was serving as a Rotary representative for Junior Achievement. I taught business and economics to the elementary-age students in Junior Achievement, and I was able to teach all three of my own kids in the process. As a Representative, you do five different sessions within a period of a few months. It looks complicated because you cover many different topics and grade levels. I was shocked to be teaching all levels from first through fourth grade, but I found I really enjoyed the contrast from litigating family law cases.

Prior Lake Rotary puts on a fairly successful music festival that draws more than 10,000 people. The acts are fairly decent. Our law firm typically sponsors this festival, and I get to jump out of my typical job and work as a bartender there in the corporate oasis tent with my husband. Our law firm also sponsors the Prior Lake Wrestling Team because my husband was a wrestler and still enjoys the sport, and a friend in Rotary asked me to support the wrestlers. My husband and I also send money to the Rotary International Foundation every year.

Involvement has grown on us in our law firm and as a family. Now the kids are so used to it that they are learning that performing charity work is one of our regular family activities. Last year, at an event through my husband's work, we helped with Hope Kids, which is an organization that helps kids who have life-threatening illnesses. In addition to being personally rewarding, doing work outside the office for the betterment of the community has a way of extending your professional reputation. Some cases come to me as a result of giving back, so I always recommend it to anybody who asks.

FINALLY

These days, especially in matters of divorce, people try to do their own legal work. I think that it's a good idea to have an attorney represent you in court but I realize it's not feasible for everyone. If you want to represent yourself, I think there is a bare minimum that every person should do. Anyone going through a divorce should at least consult with a family law attorney to understand his or her rights under the law before attempting to negotiate an agreement. It's impossible to negotiate when you don't really even know what your rights are under the law. Many people think that if they involve more lawyers then there will not be anything left except fees to pay. No one is required to hire an attorney out-right; it's possible to hire an attorney on an hourly consulting fee.

I do charge for consultations, which take between one to two hours. In a consultation, I ask many questions so that I can actually render an appropriate opinion. I tell them that if I were negotiating with this person, I would be focusing on these items.

In really valuable consultations, the attorney interviews the client thoroughly and actually tells the person the elements of his or her case, explaining what the law is and how the lawyer sees the facts in light of the law. The lawyer should provide a personal assessment of what the court may do in various situations, the trends in the law, strengths and weaknesses of the case, items that the client should emphasize, or the future path, etc. Typically I initially talk about whether the client even wants a divorce and what to expect if he or she does. The next topic tends to be the children, as the children are of paramount concern, so it is important for the client to understand the types of custody and parenting time schedules that are available and their impacts. Following the discussion about the children is typically the issue of support – how the children and spouses will be supported going forward. Other factors for discussion include the number of years of the marriage, spousal history, careers, or jobs in the past, the client's educational accomplishments versus those of the other person, and trends in the court. Lastly, it's important to review the property division and debt division, which often includes a discussion about non-marital claims and timing issues.

I think the price to pay for a consult is small compared to the risk of making a big mistake that could impact a party to a divorce for years to come. Even if a party cannot afford to retain the lawyer to represent him or her for the entire case, hopefully the client can think: "I have enough information and can negotiate for myself. I had to spend $325 or $500 for this education but at least I'm not going to leave uneducated and getting tricked." I often see people, once they have already entered into deals, who want help undoing the deal afterwards. This scenario is always much more difficult and costly than doing it right in the first place.

Without information on your rights, you'll either be negotiating in the dark or trusting someone who you likely shouldn't be trusting on the other side. That's true especially if the other party is the one who has money to lose in the deal or who will be paying for support. If the adverse party is in control of the information with a lot to lose, it is likely that he/she will do whatever is necessary to put you at a disadvantage. "Oh, you don't need a lawyer; we can just decide this between ourselves. The lawyers will take all the money. All you need is a short time to get on your feet." I've seen it all (well, maybe not all, but a lot). At a minimum, understanding your rights in family law is the best reason to do a consultation.

However, there is a huge difference in quality among family law attorneys. Some of my clients have consulted with three to five lawyers before deciding to hire me. I'll ask them, "I know you've interviewed a lot of people, why did you pick me?" I just ask the question because I'm very curious about the marketing aspect of their choice. They'll say, "It's because I didn't really get clear feedback or direction," or "They didn't break it down for me, so I didn't really understand where we were going." Many times, it seems to be more about talking and getting to know me and seeing how we connect. However, though personal connection is important, my opinion is that you're also paying money and you do want some answers. When searching for a lawyer, the smartest thing to do is to get recommendations from people you know or interact with regularly.

In family law, I am often dealing with good people who are going through one of the worst times of their lives. In family law, people arrive in my office at all different stages (the one who is leaving, the one who is left, the person scorned, etc.). Many times, people feel that they're just really overwhelmed because it's a situation they never really anticipated. They want someone asking questions to boil down everything to the essentials and frame the situation in terms that they can understand regarding what happens next or get some recommendations.

Recently our law firm overhauled our website, but we decided to stay with the same tagline that we developed when we opened our doors. Since we are good planners in times of personal crisis, we focus on having our clients develop a plan and thinking about the future, rather than dwell on past regrets. This has been a hallmark of our firm -- "Compassion, Strength, and Planning in Times of Personal Crisis." The overall theme of our content has to do with making good, practical decisions so that you can have a life after divorce. That's what we focus on because we truly care about our clients as individuals rather than just case files. It is a principle we live by. It is what gives us the privilege as attorneys to make positive differences in the lives of our clients.

(This content should be used for informational purposes only. It does not create an attorney-client relationship with any reader and should not be construed as legal advice. If you need legal advice, please contact an attorney in your community who can assess the specifics of your situation.)

3

LEAVE NOTHING
TO CHANCE

by Paul J. Dunn, Esq.

Paul J. Dunn, Esq.

Arizona Estate & Trust Law, PLC
Prescott, Arizona
www.arizonaestateandtrustlaw.com

Attorney Dunn has over 50 years experience in the planning and administration of Estates and Trusts. His law practice is devoted to private clients who want knowledgeable counsel in the areas of estate planning, estate and trust administration, and related areas of taxation. For more information on these topics please visit the Arizona Estate And Trust Law website.

Mr. Dunn was awarded his Doctorate in Law from the Ohio State University College of Law in 1964. He holds memberships in the State Bar of Arizona and its Probate & Trust Section. He served as chairman of the Probate & Trust Section of the State Bar of Arizona and was the founding editor of its Probate & Trust Newsletter. Mr. Dunn has also authored nationally published articles on estate planning and tax topics.

Arizona Estate & Trust Law, Plc is a law firm established by Prescott, Arizona Attorney Paul J. Dunn to provide individualized legal services to higher net worth Arizona residents in the areas of estate planning, estate and trust administration, and taxation.

Arizona Estate & Trust Law, Plc is committed to providing its clients with the highest quality legal services in an efficient, courteous, and dignified manner.

LEAVE NOTHING TO CHANCE

WHO IS PAUL J. DUNN?

I grew up in Tiffin, a town in north-central Ohio. Tiffin was the county seat of Seneca County and had a population of approximately 23,000. I attended Calvert High School in Tiffin and graduated as Valedictorian of my class. After graduation, I received a full scholarship to the Catholic University of America in Washington, D.C. Going from a small school to a large university and joining a campus fraternity was definitely a beneficial experience. It provided me the opportunity to meet fellow students from diverse backgrounds, to share life experiences with them, and to expand my horizons. It was quite an adjustment coming from "Small Town U.S.A."

I have been married to my wife, Carolyn, for 50 years. We met at Ohio State University in Columbus, Ohio. I was finishing law school, and she was completing her master's degree in speech pathology. I told Carolyn I would support her for the rest of her life if she would support me for five years until I could build up my law practice. She went far beyond the five years!

Our daughter is married and lives in San Diego. She is an attorney and has her own law firm. Our son is married and lives in Phoenix where he is the Senior User Experience Writer for the domain registrar GoDaddy. He has a nine-year-old daughter, who is our only grandchild. We are a close-knit family and always look forward to sharing holidays, birthdays, and anniversaries together.

LIFE CHANGERS

While I was still in college, my father passed away. I worked with his attorney in settling his estate, and that experience made me decide to become a lawyer. Originally, I planned to pursue a career in medicine, but my father's death resulted in a change of plans. Following graduation from Catholic University, I decided to attend the College of Law at Ohio State University.

Marrying my wife Carolyn was not only a significant event in my life, it was also the best decision I've ever made. Carolyn has stuck with me through thick and thin, and there have been some very thin times. She is my best cheerleader, but also my best critic. She is my proofreader and editor, and often tells me that if she can't understand something in a draft document, then other people won't understand it either. When that happens, I redraft the document to clarify its meaning and run it by Carolyn again for her approval.

Both Carolyn and I are from small towns in Ohio. At one time, our parents and all of our siblings lived within a two-hour drive from us. That made it extremely easy to get together with our family members on holidays and birthday celebrations. Nevertheless, due to our young son's severe asthmatic condition, we decided to move to Arizona. We thought our son's chance for better health was more important than proximity to our families. We chose the mile-high city of Prescott because we'd read that it was a haven for child asthmatics. This move meant I would have to begin practicing law as an unknown entity in a new location that had an entirely different property law scheme. A good friend from Ohio once told me that I was always reinventing myself. I didn't agree with her then, but I now agree — I had to reinvent my life to transition from being a solo practitioner in Ohio to becoming a solo practitioner in Arizona.

MAKING LIFE PLANS… OR NOT?

I don't believe anyone can actually "plan their life." Certain incidents lead us from one stage of life to another — stages we've never considered before. When I graduated from law school, I had no idea what area of the law I wanted to pursue. Someone suggested I consider tax law. However, that was definitely not an area of law I wanted to consider. As it turns out, my estate planning and administration practice is intimately intertwined with tax law.

After my first probate case I commented to another attorney that I didn't think probate law was an area I wanted to follow. He told me I would change my mind, and he was right. I now enjoy helping clients through all of the legal matters associated with the death of a friend or family member. I tell them I can't help with their emotional loss. However, I can make it easier for them to deal with the legalities of that loss.

I also didn't plan to live and practice law in Arizona. After graduating from college, I could have had a full scholarship to a Washington, D.C. law school. However, I decided to attend an Ohio law school because I thought I would always be practicing in Ohio. I have now spent more time practicing law in Arizona than I did in Ohio. Certainly, having a probate, trust, and tax law practice in another state wasn't something I planned for. It just happened.

Some decisions about what I would and wouldn't do have remained with me. When I first started out I handled some divorce work. My first divorce case involved an older couple who came to my office in December and wanted to get a divorce before year-end. Both of them had been divorced before and knew more about the process than I did. Moreover, their desire to be divorced was mutual, and everything went smoothly. So I thought, "This isn't so bad." I then took on two more divorce cases. Both cases involved representing mothers with young children. Unfortunately, those two cases proved to be never-ending. I had to keep going back to court to enforce child support obligation orders. After those two divorce cases were finally settled, I said to myself, "No more divorces!"

I also did criminal trial work that gave me experience in the courtroom. Although I no longer represent clients in the courtroom, that trial experience enables me to appreciate how contested probate or trust matters might play out in a courtroom. When potential clients contact me to represent them in contested matters, I decline because I want to maintain an in-office practice. Fortunately, I'm able to refer them to another attorney who does handle contested probate and trust matters. And sometimes I serve as co-counsel with that attorney.

After all these years I am often asked what kind of lawyer I am. My standard reply is, "A good one!" I then go on to say that my law practice consists of estate planning, estate and trust administration, and tax law.

MAKING THE TRANSITION: COMMUNITY PROPERTY VS. SEPARATE PROPERTY

Relocating to Arizona was a major challenge because Arizona has a totally different property law scheme than Ohio. Arizona is a community property state, whereas Ohio is a separate property state. Almost any attorney who practices in a separate property state finds the concept of community property rather daunting.

Years ago I attended seminars in Ohio where lecturers tried to explain community property concepts. However, those of us in attendance didn't see its relevance to our Ohio law practices. Of course, after moving to Arizona, I was thrust into a situation that required me to learn community property law. I soon realized that community property law dovetailed very nicely with my estate planning practice because of its tax advantages. For instance, if a husband and wife own property together as community property, both halves are revalued for tax purposes when one of them dies. In a separate property state only the deceased spouse's half is revalued. This re-evaluation is used not only for estate tax purposes, but also for future capital gains purposes.

Owning community property is definitely an advantage for people who have assets that have appreciated in value at the time of the first death. For example, if a couple in Arizona purchased an asset for $400,000 that has increased in value to $600,000 at the time of the first death, the value of that asset for both estate tax and capital gains purposes becomes $600,000. Therefore, if that asset is sold after the first death for $600,000, there would be no capital gains tax on the sale. If that same situation occurred in a separate property state, the decedent's half would be revalued at $300,000. However, the surviving spouse's half would remain at its original acquisition price of $200,000. Therefore, there would be a $100,000 capital gain on the sale if the asset was sold for $600,000 following the first death.

Owning assets as community property also makes post-death accounting and tax reporting easier by eliminating a dual depreciation schedule for investment property. This is especially helpful when a couple owns rental property, makes improvements to it over the years, and takes depreciation on it over the years. If one of them dies, that property then gets an entirely new depreciation schedule for both halves based on the property's date-of-death value.

GOING SOLO AGAIN

Moving from one state to another as a solo practitioner is extremely difficult. The best advice I can give to any attorney considering moving to another state is that if they can join an established law firm compatible with their style of practice, they should do so. That will enable them to have mentors who can share their knowledge of that state's laws and practices.

When I came to Arizona, I sought an association with one of the leading law firms in Prescott. However, that association was short-lived and turned out to be a disappointment. As a result, when I moved my family to Prescott, I did so without a job.

During those first few years we faced a lot of challenges — monetary and otherwise. However, we did survive and are thankful to be living in such a wonderful town.

REBUILDING A REPUTATION AND CLIENT BASE

After spending 20 years as an attorney in Ohio and then moving to Arizona, I knew I could transport my legal knowledge but not my reputation. Therefore, to get my name out there, I wrote weekly legal columns for the local newspaper, and I taught estate planning courses at a community college. I joined some local organizations and gave talks to lay and professional groups. I organized a Prescott estate planning group consisting of attorneys, accountants, and financial planners. I also became active in the State Bar of Arizona and lectured at bar-sponsored seminars. I served as chairman of the State Bar's Probate and Trust Law Section, and I founded its first newsletter. I was also fortunate enough to have a tax planning article authored by me published in the *American Bar Journal*.

A few years ago the Arizona Supreme Court authorized the use of trade names for attorneys. Therefore, I decided to use "Arizona Estate & Trust Law, Plc" as a trade name because it emphasized my areas of practice. Correspondingly, my office website is ArizonaEstateAndTrustLaw.com.

I have received many unsolicited offers from website developers to "improve my website to attract more clients." One of them told me my website was like an encyclopedia and certainly didn't attract clients. Shortly thereafter I received a call from a client who told me she appreciated that my website was so informative and that she was able to find an attorney who could provide the services in which she and her husband were interested. Another client told me she decided to hire me because she had perused my website, and it appeared that I knew what I was talking about.

EMBRACING TECHNOLOGY

In Ohio, I had excellent secretaries for whom I would buy the best equipment and computer programs. However, I never got involved in using the equipment or the programs. This changed when I moved to Arizona because I found myself entirely on my own in preparing documents and running my office. After six months in Arizona, I telephoned my former secretary in Ohio and proudly announced that I had found a way to practice law without her — I had learned to use a computer! To this day, I remain thankful that my father paid one of my cousins to teach me how to type when I was in high school.

I rely heavily on technology for such things as: word processing, e-mail, research, check-writing, bookkeeping, preparing tax returns, uploading encrypted documents to the cloud for client retrieval and maintaining my office website. Technology enables me to practice out of my home-office in Prescott, and it also allows me to practice from my condominium-office in Phoenix. I am able to communicate with my clients and have full access to their documents wherever I happen to be geographically.

TODAY AND THE FUTURE – CHALLENGES TO THE LEGAL PROFESSION

Everyone is aware that our society has become much more complex in every way. It stands as a corollary that the legal profession is impacted by this complexity. Attorneys not only have to keep current on the law, they also have to deliver their services in a cost-effective manner. They must do so to compete with lower-cost, non-attorney document preparation services and online legal services. Consequently, to succeed as an attorney you have to be willing to embrace change or be left behind.

When I first began practicing law, attorneys were expected to bill anywhere from 1,000 to 1,200 hours each year. Some law firms now expect their attorneys to bill double that amount. The number of hours in a day hasn't increased since I began practicing law. However, the number of hours attorneys are expected to bill has increased dramatically. This emphasis on billable hours can take a toll on an attorney's personal and family time, and every attorney must decide where the balance lies.

MANAGING A HOME-BASED LAW OFFICE

If an attorney wants to manage a law practice from home, they should first consider the type of law they want to practice. Some practices lend themselves to a home-based practice, and others do not. A probate and trust practice can be conducted quite easily from one's home because it usually involves meeting with only a few individuals at a time. However, a litigation practice requiring staff support and ongoing meetings with clients and other attorneys would be almost impossible to conduct out of a home office.

Practicing from a home office offers great flexibility. It allows you to work any hour of the day or night you find convenient. However, with that convenience, comes discipline. Working from home requires you to focus on client matters and not be distracted by household obligations. It also means you will be answering your own telephone, scheduling your own appointments, and generally (as I tell my clients) being a one-man band.

As for me, I certainly appreciate being able to have a home-based law practice. Having worked out of my home for these past many years, I can't think of practicing law any other way.

BILLING CLIENTS

After practicing for 50 years, I have observed how attorney fees have moved from one end of the spectrum to the other. When I first began practicing law in Ohio, minimum fee schedules were used for billing. These minimum fee schedules covered everything from Wills and probate matters to real estate foreclosures. However, the Federal Trade Commission considered minimum fee schedules to be "price fixing," and the U. S. Supreme Court agreed. Thereafter attorneys began charging for their services on an hourly basis. Accordingly, most attorneys kept track of the time spent by them on client matters and charged the client on the basis of hours spent.

Even though I fell in line with this paradigm shift and religiously logged my daily minutes and hours, I believed it wasn't always the best way to bill. I could spend an hour accomplishing something valuable for my clients, or I could just be spinning my wheels without imparting any value to the client. Therefore, I often reduced my fees to reflect this dichotomy. Fortunately, the trend is moving back toward fixed fees for many client services. However, there are some legal matters that are more appropriately handled on an hourly basis. Whether the fee is fixed or hourly, the important thing is that it is fair to both the attorney and the client.

In my areas of practice I believe fixed fees are a better way to bill clients because the client knows in advance the cost of the service before proceeding. I think most clients would consider this method of billing preferable to receiving an itemized statment and wondering if every item or charge on the statement was really necessary. Years ago I hired a law firm to handle a matter for me. I received a 25-page bill from them describing everything they purportedly did in resolving the matter. All I did was look at the amount due on the last page so I could pay it. I was afraid that if I thoroughly reviewed the bill to see how much time each partner, associate, and paralegal charged (and for what) I would be most unhappy.

Even though it isn't my practice to do so, many attorneys charge their clients for small "expense" items such as long-distance telephone calls, photocopies, faxes, and postage. Some law firms even place percentage surcharges on their bill instead of itemizing these expenses. Recently I received a bill from a law firm that included a 3% surcharge for "Soft Costs (Telephone, Copies, Fax, & Postage)." Interestingly, the matter was totally handled by e-mail and didn't involve any "soft costs."

MEETING THE CLIENT

My normal procedure for setting up initial appointments with prospective clients is posted on my office website. When a prospective client calls me to request an appointment, I advise them to thoroughly review my website. I want them to have some knowledge of the legal issues involved before we meet. I also want them to have an idea of the probable costs of preparing an estate plan for them.

Once the appointment is scheduled, I send the prospective clients two forms. One form is a checklist of documents and information they should bring to the appointment. The second is a form on which they can fill in their names, places and dates of birth, children's names, postal and e-mail addresses, etc. I tell them if they have any questions as they fill out the forms, they should let me know before we meet.

As posted on my website, my charge for an initial conference is $300, and a typical conference takes about two hours. At the end of the conference, I am able to tell the clients what I believe would be a suitable estate plan for them based on what they have told me. At that time I also give them a price quote to implement the estate plan I am suggesting. If they think the quoted price is fair and want to proceed, they give me a retainer that is typically two-thirds of the quoted price. If they don't think it's fair, they only owe me $300 for the time I have spent analyzing and educating them with respect to their situation. Since I began handling initial client appointments in this manner, there hasn't been a time when a prospective client has said, "It's not worth it to me."

ESTATE PLANNING – MY APPROACH

Estate planning for clients can present challenges. Some estate plans are easier to prepare than others. It is easier to prepare an estate plan for clients in their first marriage with grown children from their marriage. In this scenario, the first spouse to die usually wants the surviving spouse to have the benefit of their combined estates following the first death. And they usually want their combined assets distributed immediately and equally to their children following the second death. Estate plans get more complicated when the husband or wife (or both) have been married previously and there are multiple sets of children from those marriages. Another challenge is where the husband or wife own property they have received as an inheritance or from a previous marriage and want to keep that property as their separate property.

When I first meet with clients, I emphasize to them how the ownership of their assets is critical for two reasons. I explain that the form of ownership determines: (1) how their assets will be transferred at death, and (2) how or whether the ownership transition will be taxed. If husband and wife clients tell me they consider their assets to be equally owned by them, I suggest they consider a community property agreement. The essence of the agreement is that they consider all assets owned by them to be community property — regardless of how they acquired the assets and regardless of how the assets are currently registered.

At that first appointment I also discuss preparing the following documents in accordance with the clients' needs and desires: (1) a funded revocable trust combined with a "pour over" Will that may be needed to transfer assets to the trust following death, (2) General Powers of Attorney, and (3) Living Wills combined with Health Care Powers of Attorney.

The next step is for me to prepare drafts of these documents based on what the clients have told me. If real estate is involved, and it usually is, I also prepare drafts of deeds to transfer the real estate into trust ownership. These drafts are then sent to the clients for their review. I advise them to review the drafts very carefully and to ask me any questions they may have. I also advise them to make notes of any corrections or changes they want made to insure the documents conform to their desires. Sometimes this can be done by phone, and sometimes a follow-up office visit is required.

My estate plan documents have evolved over the years in an ongoing effort to make certain my clients truly understand them.

Nevertheless, I want my clients to tell me if there is any language in their documents they don't fully comprehend. This gives me the opportunity not only to explain the meaning of the questioned language, it also allows me to substitute a more meaningful word or phrase. Even though I pride myself on using "plain English" in all my documents, sometimes plain English can be expressed even better.

In either event, I am then able to prepare the documents in final form for signing by the clients. After the documents are signed, I scan them for my office files and give the signed originals to the clients in an indexed notebook. As part of the final office visit, I also provide the clients with a written summary of their estate plan and instructions regarding the registration and tax reporting for trust assets.

My ultimate goal in estate planning is for clients to leave my office following the signing of their documents with a sense of relief knowing their legal affairs are now in good order. I also want that same sense of relief knowing I have taken care of everything for them to the best of my ability.

WHAT YOU MAY NOT KNOW ABOUT PROPERTY OWNERSHIP

Many people mistakenly believe their Will or trust determines how all of their assets will be distributed following their death. However, the most important thing is how a decedent's assets are registered. The post-death disposition of many assets is not controlled by a Will or a trust. Instead, their disposition is controlled by contract. A Will or a trust is irrelevant if the decedent's bank or securities accounts are registered as joint tenants with rights of a survivorship or have a "payable on death" or "transfer on death" beneficiary designation. In these instances, the bank or brokerage firm doesn't care about the decedent's Will or trust. Their only responsibility is to transfer ownership of the accounts to the surviving joint tenant or to the designated account beneficiaries.

Another example of assets typically controlled by contract are life insurance policies and retirement plans such as IRAs. As long as a living beneficiary is on file with their office, the insurance company won't ask for a copy of the deceased policy-holder's Will or trust. Their contractual obligation is simply to pay the life insurance proceeds to the named beneficiary. An IRA or a company-sponsored retirement plan works the same way. The only time a decedent's Will or trust comes into play is when there is no named beneficiary on file or the named beneficiary on file is also deceased.

CHANGES IN TRUST AND TAX LAW

When I practiced law in Ohio, revocable trusts weren't immediately funded as is being done today. We waited until the client died and then funded the trust post-death by means of a "pour-over" Will filed with the probate court. It was advantageous to do so because of the tax laws in effect at that time. We would transfer income producing assets from the probate estate to the trust, and then distribute the assets from the trust to the beneficiaries. We did so in stages using different fiscal years for the estate and the trust. By so doing, a beneficiary didn't have to pay the income tax associated with the assets received by them until years later. Unfortunately Congress didn't like delayed payment of taxes by trust beneficiaries. Therefore, they amended the law to prevent trusts from using fiscal year ends. However, they allowed probate estates to continue using fiscal year ends.

Now revocable trusts are typically funded during the client's lifetime to avoid the costs associated with probate. A good thing about immediately funding a revocable trust is that it can be used to avoid a guardianship or conservatorship. If the client becomes incapacitated, it enables a successor trustee to manage the trust assets on the client's behalf without going to court. This is extremely important because if a conservatorship or guardianship is initiated the client's assets become a matter of public record. Moreover, the attorney fees and accounting fees are ongoing until the client either regains their capacity or dies. An alternate method of avoiding a court-supervised guardianship or conservatorship is for the client to have a comprehensive power of attorney. Even when I prepare trusts for clients, I also prepare companion powers of attorney as a "belts and suspenders" approach.

TELLING STORIES TO MAKE A POINT

I have accumulated a number of real life stories I rely on to help clients understand the reasoning behind the advice I am giving them. I frequently call on two such stories.

First Story: I always tell my clients not to share their estate planning documents with anyone, including family members, potential beneficiaries, or individuals they have named to administer their documents. I warn them that if they later change the distribution provisions of their documents or the individuals they have named to carry out their wishes, they may create a situation where a "disappointed" beneficiary is provided with ammunition to contest a later Will or trust. It can also lead to hard feelings if the person who thought you trusted them to carry out your wishes learns they have been replaced. To drive this point home, I tell my clients about a client who failed to follow this advice. This particular client decided to send a copy of the Will I had prepared for him to his sister for "safekeeping." Upon receiving the copy in a sealed envelope, his sister decided to unseal it and read it. She then showed the copy to their mother. The mother was so displeased with the provisions in my client's Will that she immediately had her own Will redone. As a result, my client, who was from a fairly wealthy family, was disinherited and received nothing when his mother died.

Second Story: Whenever a client wants me to draft a Will or trust that I believe may create a real problem in the future, I so advise them. However, if this is what the client really wants, it is my job to prepare the Will or trust accordingly. While I was practicing in Ohio, I encountered such a situation. The client was a woman who was not married and had no children. However, she had two sisters, both of whom had children. She owned a couple of farms she wanted to "keep in the family." She told me that when she died she wanted the farms and her entire estate to go equally to her two sisters. However, if one of her sisters died before her, she wanted her entire estate to go to the surviving sister. I advised her that could create a situation where one of her sister's children could end up with everything and the other sister's children would end up with nothing. I explained that this could result in a Will contest and create an acrimonious family situation. Nevertheless, she told me to prepare her Will as she wanted, and I agreed. However, I wrote a letter to her confirming my advice that the manner in which she was leaving her estate could cause an intra-family problem.

Sure enough, as I had envisioned and warned about, one of my client's sisters died before her. As a result, her entire estate went to her surviving sister, and the deceased sister's children received nothing. Upon learning this turn of events, the deceased sister's children planned to sue me for having prepared such a Will.

Fortunately, when they rummaged through their deceased aunt's papers, they discovered my "warning" letter and realized they couldn't sue me for preparing the Will as I did.

MEMORABLE CLIENT SUCCESSES

Although I have had many challenges during my 50 years of practicing law, three of them come readily to mind: twin criminal trials, a personal injury trial, and a federal estate tax return.

The Twin Criminal Trials: When I first began practicing law, I was court-assigned to defend a young man who, along with four of his friends, was charged with breaking and entering a tavern in the "night season." Under Ohio criminal law "night season" meant the time period before daybreak. My client's four friends pleaded guilty. My client admitted to being with his friends at the time the break-in occurred. However, he contended he didn't participate in the break-in. At the first trial my client's testimony supported my position that the incident likely occurred just after daybreak. For my closing argument, I argued to the jury that they should find my client "not guilty" for two reasons – the first being that he didn't participate in the break-in, the second being that the break-in didn't occur in the "night season." The jury was unable to reach a unanimous decision. I had hoped for a complete acquittal but was satisfied with a hung jury; I was confident the prosecuting attorney wouldn't want to retry the case.

To my surprise, the prosecuting attorney recharged my client with breaking and entering in the "day season." I was very concerned because my client's transcribed testimony made the prosecutor's new charge easier to prove. In this re-trial I argued to the jury that although my client was at the scene, he wasn't involved in the break-in and that the break-in may have occurred before daybreak. This second jury came back with a complete acquittal. One of the jurors later told me the jury thought my client was involved in the break-in, but they thought the break-in had occurred before daybreak. The Ohio legislature subsequently changed the law to eliminate the distinction between day and night for break-in offences.

The Personal Injury Trial: Early in my career, I represented a gentleman who was nearly killed in a head-on collision caused by another driver who crossed over the centerline. The driver of the other car and his passenger were killed immediately. My client suffered severe multiple injuries, was hospitalized for many months, and became permanently disabled.

I had never before tried a personal injury case, and the at-fault driver's insurance company was represented by a very experienced trial attorney. This attorney refused to even discuss an out-of-court settlement with me, thinking he could easily overwhelm me in court. Seneca County juries had a reputation for being very conservative when it came to monetary awards. Moreover, there had never been a sizable personal injury verdict in the county. After the first day of trial, when things didn't seem to be going well for the defense, the insurance company decided to make a settlement offer. My client and his wife rejected the offer, saying to me, "We want to see if you are as good as we think you are." At the end of the week-long trial, the jury returned a verdict that was roughly double the settlement offer that had been rejected by my clients and set a new county-high record for jury verdicts.

The Challenging Estate Tax Return: Recently I represented a client whose mother died leaving a sizable and very complex estate that required the filing of a federal estate tax return. The client's mother owned a number of different properties in multiple states that presented significant valuation and ownership problems. Moreover, the disposition of her mother's estate was governed by an almost incomprehensible trust document of nearly 100 pages. Before hiring me, the client had hired her mother's tax accountant to prepare the federal estate tax return.

Thirty days before the return had to be filed, my client and I decided the accountant was unable to properly prepare the return, even with my help. During those 30 days, I worked night and day to put together a nearly 300-page return to meet the filing deadline. Five and a half months after filing the return, we received an IRS notice that the return had been accepted "as filed" without an audit. I have always prided myself in having every federal estate tax return I've ever prepared accepted "as filed," even after some of them were audited due to the size of the estate or associated legal issues. However, I consider this particular return one of my most challenging and most rewarding.

SOME THOUGHTS ON PRACTICING LAW

After practicing law all these years, I have found the following snippets to be polestars of a successful law practice:

- Create daily to-do lists
- Be a problem solver
- Discuss fees up front
- Always ask clients if they have questions
- Exceed client expectations
- Keep current with changes in the law
- Continually improve your work product
- Know your limitations
- Keep your promises

- Master technology
- Have an Internet presence
- Document your advice
- Realize you can't help everyone

FINAL THOUGHTS

I try to give every client more service and attention than they expect. And when I have completed their work, I want them to feel they have received more in services than they have paid in fees. My greatest satisfaction is having clients send me thank-you notes or tell me, "You have earned every penny." Most of my clients start out as clients and end up as friends.

If anyone had told me 30 years ago that I would be practicing law out of my home without the benefit of a secretary, I wouldn't have believed them. However, practicing my type of law from my home, as I now do, has given me a tremendous amount of freedom and has been very rewarding. I wouldn't choose to switch places with anyone.

(This content should be used for informational purposes only. It does not create an attorney-client relationship with any reader and should not be construed as legal advice. If you need legal advice, please contact an attorney in your community who can assess the specifics of your situation.)

4

COAL DUST
FOR INSPIRATION:
HELPING GOOD PEOPLE
RECOVER FROM
BAD THINGS

by Joe Stanley, Esq.

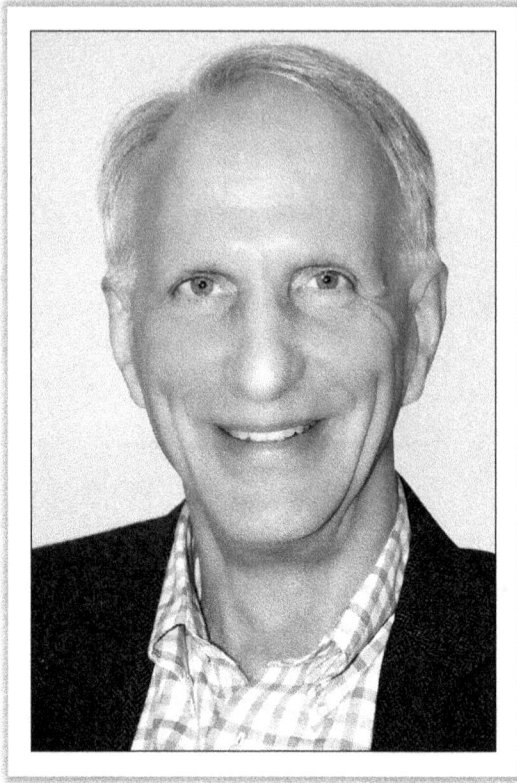

Joe Stanley, Esq.

Stanley Law
Syracuse, New York
www.stanleylawoffices.com

A native of Syracuse New York, Attorney Joe Stanley holds a Bachelor of Science Degree from the college of Environmental Sciences and Forestry and graduated Summa Cum Laude from the Syracuse University's law school in 1981. He's licensed to practice in all New York State and Federal Trial Courts. He's a member of the New York State Bar Association, Onondaga County Bar Association and the American Association for Justice. He is licensed to practice in New York, Florida, Pennsylvania, NYSLTA Academy of Trial Lawyers. He is also Board Certified in Civil Trial Practice by the American Board of Trial Advocacy.

Lawyer Stanley specializes in Personal Injury and is an advocate for the injured. He has litigated cases involving car accidents, medical malpractice, product failure, construction site injuries and more. His reputation as a meticulous litigator with a history of success is matched by his ability to connect with his clients personally while fighting for their compensation. He lives in Skaneateles, New York with his wife, two sons and a daughter.

Coal Dust For Inspiration: Helping Good People Recover From Bad Things

Of Heroes And Their Champions

There are heroes among us. They may not be the unstoppable kind of caped heroes you're used to seeing at a movie theater. They drive a tractor-trailer, work at a school or steel mill, and have families and neighbors. These heroes are real. Here at Stanley Law we call them our clients, our friends.

In the real world the story of a personal injury attorney is not a glamorous one, at least mine isn't. It's a difficult yet rewarding privilege. I defend those who cannot defend themselves. Seeking justice for those who rightfully deserve it and giving these heroes a voice is our number one priority. When the heroes feel no one else is listening, when they can't go it alone, we're there for them. It's what we do every day across Upstate New York and Pennsylvania.

But for the grace of God go any one of us. A serious injury can rip your life apart in an instant. No one is immune. What we do here is serious work, often with very sad, even tragic circumstances. It's important work, especially against today's odds posed by the insurance companies and the system. I sometimes wonder if I had the opportunity whether I would do it all over again. Even heroes need help; so I roll up my sleeves and get to work, reminding myself, yes, this is what I was born to do.

THE EARLY YEARS

Born and raised in Syracuse, New York, I suppose you have ingrained in your DNA a certain tenacity. The elements here can be harsh, sometimes unforgiving. As a kid I lived in the suburbs. I remember being around seven or eight years old, taking the bus into the city to go to the dentist or doing whatever seemed fun at the time. I used to ride my bike everywhere! Things for kids and parents sure have changed a lot since then.

Hard work was always a requirement growing up, thanks to my father and grandfather, who instilled a good work ethic in me from an early age. I had my first paper route at nine years old. I used to spend a few weeks in Pennsylvania every year with my grandfather Joseph, who I was named after. A coal miner who'd emigrated from Lithuania, my grandfather retired due to black lung disease, also known as "miner's asthma." He raised chickens and grew plants, saving every penny to give savings bonds to all of his grandchildren. Grandfather insisted we were never going to do what he did, that we were going to get educated. He would say if we didn't get educated he didn't want to know us. He wanted all of his children and grandchildren to go to school and make something of ourselves. Nearly all of the seven kids and all of us grandchildren put ourselves through college. It wasn't easy back in those days. You didn't get scholarships and there was no government aid.

Before World War II my father worked in the coal mines for five years and then went into the Army. I still remember him spitting up coal dust when I was growing up. After the military, working full-time and earning his Bachelor of Science in Industrial Relations, he ultimately ran the General Electric union in Syracuse for 25 years. He contracted multiple myeloma, probably from all the years of chemical exposure on the line at GE. Over 17,000 employees were under my dad's care during his 24/7 job. It was a never-ending battle to help people. That's just the way life was in the Stanley household, all I ever really knew. It was a time I will never forget. I was 7 or 8 years old and there was a long strike. Someone fired a gunshot through our front window. My father just kept trying to do what he thought was right to get the employees a better wage and benefits. Because of our family's dedication to helping people, it only seemed natural that I would go into personal injury law.

My dad sent me to Christian Brothers Academy where I did *not* want to go. Although it was probably better for me, I didn't like it. It was all the way across town and a 45 minute ride to the bus connection so I wasn't able to do any extracurricular things after school, because it was too far away. Without sports I still kept busy during high school. I always worked.

Work was definitely part of the routine. So when I headed off to college at SUNY College of environmental science and forestry in Syracuse, I truly enjoyed the experience. I learned a lot and got my Bachelor's degree in Science. I then finished my whole Master's degree program in one year at the University of Binghamton. With a flood of offers for me to go to PhD programs, the great recession in the 70's hit, so instead I took the LSAT. It was kind of a joke because I didn't even get a book! I just read the instructions when I took the exam and luckily did pretty well. I graduated first in my law school class.

Initially I went to law school with the idea I wanted to do environmental law. I quickly determined it was too boring for me and wasn't at all what I wanted to do. I got into personal injury because I thought it would enable me to use a lot of my technical scientific background. I knew a lot of science, anatomy, and biochemistry. More than half of what a personal injury attorney does is a combination of medicine, science, and the law. For me, it was a good fit.

Personal injury law keeps me busy and it's always changing. I get bored easily if I'm doing the same repetitive things that lack challenge. Personal injury work is very challenging. Whether it's a car crash or a construction accident, a medical malpractice case or a nursing home neglect or abuse case, every case and each person is different.

Personal injury cases are always unique, especially in New York. A relatively minor variation in cases can make the difference between the offer of compensation in the negligence type of case, or the situation where you just have to use your own resources. If you don't have your own resources than that's a huge problem; a lot of people have no safety net. Lacking your own disability or health insurance, or having a significant personal injury, can really disrupt your financial and emotional situation.

Seeing bad things happen to good people is the very difficult side of my work. As a personal injury attorney you have to keep faith and trust that you're making a difference for the right people when they need you most. It's the thing that keeps you going each day in the face of tremendous sadness. Our clients are the real heroes and they inspire us to continue to do the work and fight the good fight.

People think when they need a personal injury lawyer they won't be able to afford it. Personal injury lawyers are not like most of the attorneys the people imagine, we are there to protect our clients. We're only compensated as personal injury attorneys if a client wins a settlement. So as the firm representing a client, we have a good deal of skin in the game too... a lot of cost, time and energy are invested in an effort to ensure the right outcome, for the client first and foremost, and then of course for our firm.

THE FUTURE OF PERSONAL INJURY LAW

You have to embrace change. I always look five years down the road. If I hadn't always been planning ahead, I'm not sure I would be where I am now. Change is happening so rapidly in the world I almost feel like I have to run to catch up at times. This type of law practice is going to change. Cars are going to go faster, however there will be fewer accidents because companies are making cars safer, and fairly soon computers will be driving cars. Maybe by then, people will be suing Google or Yahoo. To some degree I'm kidding, but that's the change that's happening around us.

A particular area of interest for our firm has is protecting those people who are in nursing homes or senior living facilities. In essence we are their voice and the voice of their families. Nursing home abuse and neglect is on the rise and it's despicable the lack of quality care, training and compensation for these nursing homes staffs. The staffs are under-trained and under-staffed. Period. There are models of excellence. Nursing home operators who are indeed getting it done and done well. That's the model that all should be held accountable to.

People are getting older, living longer, and the challenge of finding good, quality, long-term care for our aging population, will become more, not less than it is today. The problem is most definitely not going away. It's part of my mission and vision to educate people about the level of neglect and abuse that occurs. There's so much that needs to be done. Our parents and grandparents are simply getting tossed aside. More advocates must demand the standard of care increase and facilities be held accountable. Our elders deserve nothing less than dignity and kindness, compassion and loving care.

Another area that absolutely requires change is the medical malpractice system. In fact, the healthcare system in general is terrible. It's clearly not at the level it should be, mostly because doctors want to make money instead of following the "do no harm" principle. Unfortunately that notion is a lost dream. Despite the amount of malpractice, our firm has to limit the number of cases we can undertake. I restrict malpractice cases to probably 10% of our business. I have to turn down far too many every month. Based on the current system, although the individual may clearly have a case, I have to tell them that due to the way the system's set up, we can't help them. It's very hard. It costs more to pursue the case than can be won, and the chances of winning are not that good.

You have to be wary of our healthcare system. Be diligent. Be your own best advocate. Talk with people who are in the know, like any good personal injury lawyer who knows the pitfalls and the tactics of the system. The gamble is just too high to try and go it alone.

GOVERNMENT AND HEALTH CARE – A PORTENTOUS PARTNERSHIP

The intertwining of government and healthcare, I think, is going to hurt lawyers and those seriously injured. For some reason people hold this belief that lawyers are somehow causing the system to cost more than it should, which isn't true. We're always trying to get this message out to lawyers that right now the way the government is run, in particular, the way that some politicians want the system to change, makes the system hard to deal with. If you took lawyers out of the mix for products, drugs prop, and malpractice, the entire system would run amok. Without lawyers, there would be more people injured without any remedy. All of these injured people would be tossed aside while others made millions in profits.

For example, go back and analyze lawnmowers, washing machines, or dryers from the 1970s until the present. They're so much safer now, so are automobiles. Essentially anything that's manufactured is safer today! The reason these products are safer is because of lawyers, not because of the government.

For healthcare, there's nobody policing doctors; they're supposed to be policing themselves, but they aren't. If you bring claims against hospitals and doctors, with no impetus to be better, you're just penalizing the poor innocent people who are the repository of the negligence. You can't rely on the government because they can only work generally; specifically, it's not going to help anyone in his or her individual situation.

Health insurance is even harder to deal with. The medical loss ratios with health insurance kick in if there's a treatment that's not covered, the treatment that the insurance company doesn't think you need, or if the company wants you to accept only substandard care they're willing to pay for. I've experienced this personally.

Recently I hurt my neck playing basketball. I don't like going to doctors because I know how crazy the medical system can be, and I sue doctors. The doctor wanted to prescribe Celebrex for my treatment; as you may know it's a sort of super Advil. When I called about the treatment, the insurance company wouldn't approve the medication. Instead they wanted me to get some very expensive injections, which don't really work by the way. The insurance company wouldn't approve Celebrex until I had injections - even though the medicine cost a fraction of the cost of the injections. It was absurd! I had to go through a gauntlet to get approval for Celebrex. The company did approve it but only after I threatened to sue them.

A word of advice: do not simply accept and follow the advice of your insurance company without consulting a personal injury attorney. The care that the insurance company recommends is often different from the care the injured person truly requires. If you get a recommendation or referral for a really good doctor to help with the disability or injury, you have a lot better chance of recovery. When you leave the hospital, don't just visit the first recommended specialist offered by the insurance company.

THE PROVING GROUND – THE COURTROOM

I've tried a lot of cases over the years. I'm a member of the American Board of Trial Advocates (ABOTA), and you can't be a member unless you've tried numerous cases. In personal injury law if you don't try cases, you can never resolve cases, because the insurance companies will just ignore you if you don't have that kind of leverage in your history. When you lose a case you look at the reasons why, and sometimes you learn more from losing than winning. You not only have to learn to lose, but you have to adapt and educate yourself. I've been using focus groups for what seems like forever because it's a way of developing cases. I try to use as many of the theories out there as possible, like the Reptile strategy, the approached developed by Don Keenan and David Ball. There's a combination of ways to get your message across in the proper manner, and filling in the scientific background has become far more sophisticated.

Many lawyers say they don't lose, but that's impossible; just like any lawyers who say they did it all on their own. I have to thank hundreds of people who've worked for and with me over the years and helped me become successful; without them I certainly wouldn't be where I am today.

When I first became a lawyer, what was believed then and what we know now is so different. It's incredible the way the litigation process has changed. Eric Oliver is one of my favorites - I still have his first book, *The Facts Can't Speak for Themselves* – I still use that book today. I've probably read it 15 times and still try to learn more from it every day. Trying cases is very sophisticated, very expensive and very time-consuming; it can only be done by taking the best of the approaches and making cases better. Learning new approaches is an important part of change. I attend and teach seminars because I love to learn; and continual learning, especially in my business, is crucial.

Now that I've been attorney for so long, when I speak to new clients I have a vision. I can see in my mind, at least with a good probability, how the case will pan out. You become meticulous but you can always be surprised by some sort of change, because you don't have enough information. We work to educate our clients that complete disclosure upfront with us could mean the difference between winning and losing a case. As a best practice, a lawyer has to meet with any client in detail before even signing with them, no matter how simple the case may seem.

MY FIRM'S FOUNDATION

Together with my team, we've developed an approach that's important to our work and our success. The four cornerstones we rely upon at Stanley Law are: We always challenge every insurance company's denial. We always research every case. We always enlist the best specialists in the state. We always investigate every delay. Our promise to clients is to leave no stone unturned. Always.

As with any profession there are a lot of bad attorneys; they're probably could be fewer. An attorney must be a positive influence in peoples' lives. You have to be knowledgeable and helpful, because the people you're helping are at a critical stage in their lives. Not just in personal injury law but in any area of law; these people are going through a traumatic time whether their particular situation is a divorce, injury, accident, or estate planning - it's all important. You have to truly care and have an immense amount of empathy in this business.

As I touched upon earlier, I've had the tremendous pleasure of working with some really good people. My partner has been with me since he was a law clerk, and three associates have been since the beginning of their careers. You have to work hard and be thorough. Your clients, the insurance company, and the defense lawyers have to know you're going to do a good job and pursue your cases with tremendous tenacity. Once you take on the case they have to know that you're in it to the finish and that you're in it to win it! I think that's a valuable reputation to have.

I've taken some really difficult cases over the years because I'm not afraid to win or lose; I've never been afraid to lose, even though I don't particularly like it. I don't know of any lawyer or anyone who does! If you don't lose, you're not taking the hard cases. I don't like to spend the money on hard cases, but it's an educational process that's necessary. It also means you're telling the defense lawyers and insurance companies you are willing to take a chance for the people who deserve it, whether they think so or not.

I have a philosophy I follow - Death to Excuses. I don't want to hear excuses; I just want to hear solutions. It's important to figure out what you did wrong to make sure you don't do it again. I'm a firm believer in this phrase: when in doubt, check it out.

I also stay active. I run, play basketball, and go to the gym five or six days a week. It not only keeps me physically fit but mentally fit as well. Exercise is one of my keys to sanity.

A Culture Of Public Service

A primary focus of our firm is education because without it people have no true sense of what is and what's possible. Public service is a key component in all that we do. As an example I'll be adding law students to the firm soon and they'll have to do pro bono work as well. I personally spend a lot of time doing community pro bono work myself, answering legal questions, speaking at the local rescue mission monthly, simply to give counsel to those who need help and hope. Part of our awareness initiative utilizes local radio shows in the communities where people call in with legal questions. I host a television show once a month as well. In some cases we get so many calls during a half hour show the lines are full and the station can't get in their advertisements! People send me emails after the show too. I get a great deal of enjoyment out of it and I also know it's an important part of what we do.

MUSIC FOR THE MISSION

Several years ago I decided to take the charitable work that I was doing with the local rescue mission organization and couple that with music to get people in the community involved with people who are hungry and homeless. I had a couple of relatives who had problems with alcohol a long time ago. There was very little support not only for alcoholism but for homelessness and joblessness which was even less than it is now.

I understand any one of us is often only one step away from being in that situation, and hopefully, if I were stuck in that situation, there would be somebody who would be able to help me out. That's really the reason we started music for the mission. It's all voluntary. And all those who volunteer agree we should help people who are less fortunate. It's just the right thing to do.

Even today as a lawyer, I represent people that live on the edge. In fact they were probably living on the edge before the serious injury and their accident simply puts them into a financial and emotional abyss. As much as we are lawyering for our clients, we're as often confidantes and counselors.

Today, I'm married with three children. I am an incredibly proud dad. All three of my kids went to Cornell University as undergraduates. My oldest son went on to law school at Stanford University, graduating at the top of his class. He now lives and works in Philadelphia. My daughter got her Master's in public health and works in the healthcare field in San Francisco. My youngest son is going to school to be a nurse practitioner next fall.

It's been almost twenty years since my dad passed away, I know he'd be proud. I'm certain my grandfather Joseph would be too.

LOOKING AHEAD

As I begin to write my next chapter in life and in business, I hope to continue the good works that I'm proud this firm has had a hand in. Defending the true heroes, the clients, who deserve to be heard and deserve their justice, is what we shall always champion. Raising awareness and demanding change within our nursing home and assisted living facilities is important work that I'll be leading over the next many years. For as long as it takes to ensure that the standard of care is raised and the neglect and abuse is eliminated, we will fight the good fight. Our elders deserve dignity. If we can have a hand in ensuring that more of that happens across New York State, and the country for that matter, then I'll know that all our efforts have been worth it.

There are indeed heroes among us. The Team at Stanley Law, my law firm partner Rob Quattrocci, myself, are all proud to know and help them.

(This content should be used for informational purposes only. It does not create an attorney-client relationship with any reader and should not be construed as legal advice. If you need legal advice, please contact an attorney in your community who can assess the specifics of your situation.)

5

FAMILY FIRST:
LESSONS IN LOVING

by Kim Boyer, Esq.

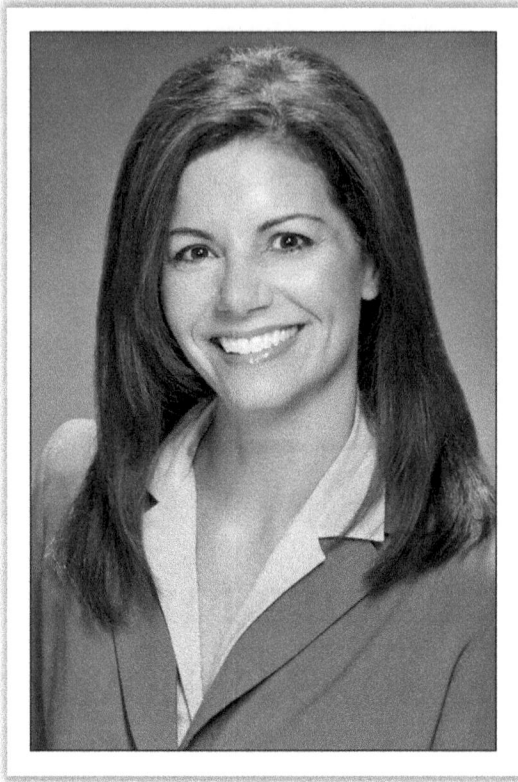

Kim Boyer, Esq.
Boyer Law Group
Las Vegas, Nevada
www.elderlawnv.com

Counselor Boyer is Certified as an Elder Law Attorney by the National Elder Law Foundation. She practices in the areas of elder law, estate planning, guardianships and probates. Ms. Boyer received her A.B. degree in Mathematics, summa cum laude, from San Diego State University, and her law degree magna cum laude, from the University of San Diego School of

Law. During law school, she was an editor of the law review and was elected to membership in the Order of the Coif.

Ms. Boyer is licensed to practice in Nevada, and is admitted to the U.S. District Courts for the District of Nevada and the Ninth Circuit Court of Appeals. She is a member of the National Academy of Elder Law Attorneys, the National Guardianship Association, and is an accredited attorney with the Veterans Administration. She is co-author of the book Alzheimer's and Dementia: A Practical and Legal Guide for Nevada Caregivers, published by the University of Nevada Reno Press. Ms. Boyer publishes a monthly newsletter addressing issues facing seniors and their families, and is a frequent speaker on aging and elder law topics.

FAMILY FIRST: LESSONS IN LOVING

I was born and raised in San Diego, where I attended undergraduate and law school. During school I was on law review with a student whose father was a prominent attorney in Las Vegas. She told me that Las Vegas was an amazing place to practice law and encouraged me to come to Las Vegas. During law school, I clerked for a law firm in Las Vegas and they offered me a position upon graduation. So many people cannot believe that I left the beautiful beaches of San Diego for the desert, yet I have found Las Vegas to be a great place to practice law. With my husband and son and family life, I feel blessed beyond measure.

MY MOTHER'S MIGHTY INFLUENCE

I am often asked why I became an elder law attorney. My mother taught me to be strong, self-reliant, and independent, and she would generally let me make my own decisions. From an early age, if I asked permission to spend the night at a friend's house, my parents would let me decide – it was my choice. Because of her influence, I was able to decide whether my request was really the best idea.

She also told me, "Get an education so you don't have to rely on a man–be independent." She was always stressing the importance of education, and at the early age of eight years old, I made the commitment to get a good education. Later on, I became a valedictorian in high school, my grades allowed me to get Summa Cum Laude for my undergraduate degree, and I graduated Magna Cum Laude from law school.

After I decided to go to law school, many people told me that I was too kind to be an attorney. I knew that I could find an area in which compassion counted as a strength for an attorney, not a weakness, partly because my mother taught me that I could do whatever I was determined to do. After law school, I was blessed to get a job working for an extraordinary attorney, who is now a Nevada Supreme Court justice. She taught me about excellence and professionalism. One case we worked on together, the opposing counsel requested multiple extensions. Calmly and with grace, she granted him the extensions, saying that you freely grant continuances if it does not harm your client. It was a simple act, yet it stayed with me all these years that we have many opportunities to do things with grace or professionalism. And that opposing counsel sent me referrals years later, so you never know how your professionalism can benefit you in the future. She also expected the highest caliber work product and set the bar high. I think of her high standard of excellence and work to hold myself to that level.

WHY ELDER LAW?

My undergraduate degree is in mathematics. I love solving problems. Though I obtained a job as an engineer, it was not what I wanted to do for the rest of my life. I really did not want to sit in a cubicle. When I talked with my supervisor, telling him that I wanted more interaction with people, he looked at me and said, "Well, talking is not in the job description." After spending some time analyzing careers that would make use of my problem-solving skills while interacting with people, and after much consideration, I eventually chose the law. It allows me to be compassionate, talk with people, and counsel people in my own way.

Even though my first job in a law firm let me work for a great attorney – the Nevada Supreme Court justice – I also knew that litigation was not what I truly wanted to do. One day, as I was working at my desk reading the incoming mail, I saw a brochure from the National Academy of Elder Law Attorneys describing their upcoming seminar in Las Vegas. As I read it, I decided to take it in. While attending the seminar, I made up my mind quickly to become an elder law attorney and devote my career to serving the elderly. The other attendees' conversation, in the way they talked about elder law as a way to help vulnerable people during a challenging time in their lives, really solidified my decision. One piece of incoming mail changed the direction of my life. A purpose does not have to come to you in a dramatic way, and you might miss it if you are only looking for life-changing moments among the bells and whistles.

Whether a loved one is sick or a spouse has just died, circumstances look different when you are in pain or nearing the end of life. As an attorney who helps the elderly and their families, I have heard thousands of stories about the elements that make up a good life or lead to pain. I have learned about what people deeply long for, what they fear, and what matters most in the end.

Some of my clients come in when things are good to get their affairs in order. Others are at a point in their lives when they are experiencing a low level of happiness. Many of my clients are either sick or dying, or their loved one is sick or dying. They worry about grief and loss and about medical bills – how bills will jeopardize their financial security. Part of elder law includes knowing the laws to help these people, but I'm also able to come in and provide support for them on multiple levels.

Beyond taking care of matters from a legal standpoint, I'm also another human being who interacts with the family. I can do things that will increase their happiness level; it's not just what I say, but how I say it. I feel that I've been made for this profession and I feel blessed, every day, to do what I do.

LIFE – AN ONGOING ADVENTURE

I see many people who suffer and then give up or stop trying. Don't stop using the power you have. Start a business, take up fencing, or learn another language. Do whatever calls to you.

It is amazing when you have people in your life who offer valuable guidance. After I accomplished something, I would want to immediately share it with my Mom. She'd briefly celebrate, then immediately begin asking questions to push me to the next level. My Mom said, "Think big and you'll get bigger." At times, this felt uncomfortable. Big goals can seem unattainable at first, yet there was the drive to live up to the level she set.

If you don't have someone inspiring you and driving you, find someone who will, or do it for yourself. Also, remember the times you set out to do something that seemed like a stretch, only to discover with delight that you were able to do it. Sometimes goals are easier to achieve than you might imagine, and sometimes they are harder. On the journey, you can grow if you extend yourself.

I constantly learn from my clients. I learn about their lives and the lessons that they've learned - what happened to them, and what they would have done differently. I take those educational moments from my clients and integrate them into my own life, and then use those lessons to help other people.

SECRETS OF A BRIGHTER LIFE

People who build wonderful and successful lives have some things in common. They have enviable attitudes and values; they will embrace every opportunity to grow and learn. They live a healthy lifestyle, work hard, enjoy life, don't tend to worry, and are religious (in a broad sense.) Most have a strong will to live fully, and a high appreciation for the simple experiences and pleasures of life. Bad things may happen in their lives, but they are adaptable and resilient.

As I walked into Jesse's room at the assisted living facility, I saw that she was a tiny lady, smiling and reading the morning newspaper. Her eyes looked clear and alert, and radiated with joy. Her mind was sharp, much sharper than many of the residents at the facility. At age 98, she had moved past her biological probability. With a glow in her face, she said, "I've lived a long and wonderful life. My time is near and I want to get my affairs in order. I take good care of myself. I eat right, don't smoke or drink, and exercise daily. I pray, as it gives me balance. I stayed connected with my family. The most important thing was thinking about what to do next, to have a plan and a purpose. My great Aunt Dorothy inspired me. She lived to be 99. She got up and worked in the garden every morning. Everyone told her to stop working, but she loved working and the feel of the soil. She was nimble, independent, and self-reliant."

DON'T STOP THINKING AHEAD

Can you imagine what you will want and what you will be like on the day that you turn 100 years old? Will you say that your life was wonderful? Many people would answer that they want a sharp mind, to remain healthy, to be active, and have a purpose.

Whether or not you desire longevity, nobody wants to spend their years in poor health. You can change your future, starting today, by adopting attitudes that will help you thrive. When you are engaged in your own life, you trigger a cascade of reactions that light up the brain. The intense repetition of a task creates new and stronger neural pathways. As a person becomes an expert in a particular area, the areas of the brain associated with those skills actually grow. You can promote this brain remodeling by exposing yourself to new experiences and learning new skills.

With Alzheimer's disease, one of the first things to indicate decline is the loss of short-term memory. The key neural projections that allow for the storage of sensory information are severed from a build-up of neurotoxic beta-amyloid. Then, nerve endings begin to shrink and break down in the same region. The result is devastating. The person with Alzheimer's suffers along with their loved ones. Even the early stages are frightening. It is often the end of the dream of a long, vital, and loving life.

The reality of Alzheimer's can be used as a goal for creating a better life. Behavior shapes biology. Research shows that positive lifestyle changes in diet, exercise, stress management, and meditation affect the human genetic code. Your lifestyle can potentially trump your genetic predisposition, and you can take steps to prevent disease. This is a gift to those you love.

EIGHT KEYS FOR IMPROVING YOUR LIFE AT ANY AGE

1. **Add to the sweetness in your life and reduce that which does not feel good.** Make the time to do more of those things that bring you joy and pleasure. Cut out those activities that do not leave you feeling good. You can learn to listen to your body as it expresses itself through signals of comfort or discomfort. Some of the signals are subtle and some more obvious, yet as you learn to listen to those signals and take action, you can move toward more sweetness, and away from that which does not feel good. You may learn to ask your body to tell you how it feels about a certain behavior or choice. If your body sends a signal of emotional or physical distress, watch out. If it sends a signal of comfort or eagerness, proceed. If you spend more time in silence or in meditation, quieting the internal dialogue, you can become more aware of the subtle signals. (Some call this "intuition.") As you pay attention to your inner life, you can be guided by this intuition rather than the externally imposed limitations on what is or isn't good for you.

2. **Act out of love whenever you can.** Be compassionate. When you operate from love and compassion, rather than judgment, you feel an amazing sense of lightness. Everything can be understood and forgiven, and when you

judge, you cut off that understanding and shut down the process of letting love in. Learn to replace fear-motivated behavior with love-motivated behavior. Fear comes from memory of past hurts and it creates strong impulses to avoid pain. Yet, when you focus on keeping a past hurt from repeating itself, you don't avoid that fear. You may even re-create it. To remove that fear of hurt, find the security within yourself, which is love. When you are moved by love, you can face fears because you come from a place of true inner strength. When you act from love, do not question or seek external approval for your actions. There is great freedom in this.

3. **Be calm within yourself.** Thoroughly accept what comes to you; learn from it, then let it go. Look for the fullness in every moment. Don't struggle with what is, because the present is as it should be.

4. **Create good thoughts and use good words.** The thoughts that you think and the words that you speak will create your experiences. Studies have shown that the cells in your body are affected by your every thought. Thoughts show a real impact in your feelings and behaviors. Negative thoughts are like pollution in your system. Unfortunately, most of us have learned to think about what we *don't* want. Begin a practice of dropping, or ignoring, the negative and fearful thoughts that enter your mind. As they come into your mind, gently, but firmly, let them go. As they return, let them go again. Do this again and again, until they are gone. Life becomes healthier without those thoughts. Then, begin a practice of thinking about what you *do* want. You might be thinking about something that you believe is lacking in

your life. It's possible to choose to rethink that belief in order to concentrate on how much you do have.

5. **Add to peaceful interactions.** Be tolerant. When you find yourself reacting with anger or opposition to a person or situation, realize that you are just struggling with yourself and even harming yourself. Anger and other toxic emotions contaminate your body, sometimes even more than bad foods. The health of every cell directly contributes to your state of well-being. Putting up resistance is often the response to past hurts. When you eliminate that response, you heal yourself and become more able to help others.

6. **Be of service.** Service begins with empathy. Empathy means being involved enough to understand the needs of others and how you can help with those needs. Empathy means exchanging judgment for understanding - and taking action. You can cultivate empathy by listening carefully to those words that are spoken and to those that remain unspoken. Giving is most appreciated when you give what is actually needed, not what you think is needed. Understanding what is needed can come from learning to listen with empathy. By listening more carefully, you can begin to hear the needs of humanity. You can begin to understand more fully how your hands can be the hands that change a human life.

7. **Let life touch you.** Many of us just let the good stuff of life roll on by. Instead, you can take something good and let it affect you in a way that will reshape your brain. If you savor the positive experience, feel positive emotions, and allow them to soak in, you can reshape your brain into a better framework. For instance, I often sit in my

library with the morning sunlight streaming in through the window. There is a hummingbird just outside the window, tasting the delicate rosemary flowers. As I soak in this simple beauty, I feel gratitude and joy. The next time that you see a beautiful bird, flower, or laughing child, spend at least 20 seconds soaking it in with joy. The more emotion you feel, the more you will light up your brain and create new pathways that enable you to experience the good more often.

8. **Do the right thing.** You can choose to do the right thing and then do the next right thing. Over time, these actions add up. Then, you follow an upward curve, no matter what age you are. When you become enthusiastic or add other positive emotion, it intensifies this process.

CULTIVATING JOY

For some people, a stroke or a heart attack is the catalyst that gives them reason to create lasting change. The event scares them, and they want to make sure that they do more for their spouse, children, or grandchildren in their remaining days. Don't wait until you suffer a major illness. Start making healthy choices now, and living the life you are meant to live.

Many people only experience fleeting moments of happiness and temporary states of well-being, rather than lasting happiness. The happiest people show these behaviors: practicing gratitude, and positive thinking, investing in social connections, managing stress and trauma, living in the present, committing to goals, and taking care of their body and soul. Happy people do have stress and crises, but they show poise and strength in the face of such challenges.

My Mom always said that life is not made of the extraordinary things, or the big moments, but the little things. Many of us get caught up in thinking that we need something extraordinary to feel joyful. In listening to my clients talk about their lives, it is clear that their most precious memories come from a collection of ordinary, everyday moments. Stop long enough to be grateful for those moments and the joy they bring.

I am inspired on a daily basis by those ordinary moments; like watching the sun glisten on the trees, laughing at work, sharing a meal, or reading by the fireplace. Knowing that life is really about these moments has changed my life and turned the ordinary into the extraordinary. Gratitude brings grace, a spontaneous joy, and zest for life, love, and so much more.

DAILY WAYS TO ENGAGE IN ORDINARY MOMENTS

- Keep a gratitude journal, in which you can write down those things for which you are grateful.

- Write handwritten notes of appreciation, telling people why you are grateful for them.

- Say out loud to yourself; "I am grateful for ____."

- When you see something beautiful, take more time to stop and look at it, and find words to express how that beauty enriches your life.

- Take every opportunity to tell others what you appreciate about them.

- Relish ordinary experiences like eating a meal or taking a shower. Instead of rushing through or thinking about all of the things you need to do next, just be in the moment and savor what you are experiencing right now.

- Reminisce with others about something you shared together, with the intent of transferring that joy from the past into the present. It is especially important for older people to extract positive feelings from reminiscence.

- Open yourself to the beauty of nature. Gaze at the stars, enjoy the sunset or sunrise, admire plants and flowers, and look at the tiny details of that flower that you ordinarily don't see. Take time to listen to the birds, and marvel at the beauty of the wind in the trees. Strive to feel reverence and awe.

- Take pleasure in the senses. Feel the sun warm your skin, breathe in the fresh morning air, walk barefoot on the beach, or savor the aroma of fresh bread.

- Listen to music and dance with abandon.

Take the time to cultivate the overall sense of joy in your life. Don't let it slip, regardless of the complexity of your life. Be grateful for what you do have and savor the goodness in those things. Expect to be greeted by a flood of joy when you are surrounded by nature, when you throw yourself into a work project, or when you laugh and sing.

RECOVERY THROUGH RESILIENCE AND COMPASSION

"This is just too much pain," said my client Richard, trying to fight back the tears. His wife was in the hospital following a stroke. Her prognosis was not good. They'd been together for forty years, and he could not imagine life without her.

Everyone encounters stress, adversity, grief, or crisis. Some people never recover. Others eventually get back to the place where they were. Some come back even stronger. What makes some people never recover and others bounce back? *Emotional resilience* is the ability to bounce back after something bad happens, and it is also a strong indicator of longevity.

Resilient people ask for help, maintain good social support and connections, tap into emotional resources, and are good at solving problems. When you suffer, you can feel a range of negative emotions: fear, sadness, pain, guilt, and hopelessness. To get through that type of suffering, it is important to have a belief in something greater than human beings – a force with the capacity to heal.

As a society, we don't allow much time for sadness and grieving. We urge people to "get over it" and take a pill to hurry along the process. However, suppressed grief will find its way to expression, and quite often in a harmful way. Hurrying through grief means that we fail to understand the lessons grieving has to teach us.

If you've gone through a challenging time and raised yourself back up, you arise with new power. You will speak with more credibility because you have endured and moved beyond the valley of suffering. You will experience more compassion for others who suffer because you know first-hand how much it hurts. Having gained wisdom and humility, you will be more prepared to serve.

Sometimes your words to someone else can make an incredible difference. A kind word, listening with an open heart, or sharing your story may be just what that person needs. As an elder law attorney, I sit with people in my office, or sometimes in their living rooms, or at their hospital bed, in the middle of a crisis. I solve legal issues, yet there is more to it than that. We talk about their lives, wonderful things, and simple things. I listen with an open heart, and often times I am able to help them legally. Yet the most amazing part is that I end up feeling blessed by them.

Serving others is a blessing to both the giver and the receiver. You can serve in many ways, through acts of encouragement, kindness, and hope. As the cycle repeats itself, you will find yourself moving into wider spheres of blessing, spiraling upward. When you shine your light, you make it easier for others to shine their lights, so the world becomes a brighter place.

FINDING THE RIGHT ELDER ATTORNEY

I am a member of the National Academy of Elder Law Attorneys, and am certified as an elder law attorney by the National Elder Law Foundation. Attorneys who have attained that certification have gone through a rigorous process, and have the knowledge base to address legal issues affecting the elderly and their families. I would encourage anyone who needs an elder law attorney to choose a certified elder law attorney. If there are multiple certified elder law attorneys in your area, then interview them until you find the one who makes you feel most comfortable. It's important to choose someone who fits well with your own personality. You need to be able to feel completely at ease with your legal counsel.

Most elder law is state-specific; only a few areas include federal law. My firm meets with clients in Nevada or Las Vegas. Many retirees move to Las Vegas while their families live elsewhere. When the retiree in Las Vegas becomes ill or frail, their family members who live out-of-state need help in getting their estate and accounts in order, so the out-of-state family members often hire our firm to help the in-state resident. Each case depends on its own circumstances.

If you need an elder law attorney, especially for someone in a long-term care facility or hospital, one of the best ways to find such an attorney is a word-of-mouth referral from other people staying at the same facility. You can also go online and search the National Academy of Elder Law Attorneys website, naela.org, for certified elder law attorneys in your particular city or community, as well as asking around in your community for person-to-person referrals.

BEFORE YOUR CONSULTATION

People who are referred to my office or search online usually call our office. My amazing staff has been with me for many years; one staff member has been at the firm for 19 years, two others for 14 years, and so on. We all love what we do - helping people with compassion, making a difference. So when someone calls us, my wonderful staff asks that person a series of questions just to get a picture of the situation. If it looks like we could actually help, then we'll set up the consultation free of charge. Sometimes people call and there just isn't anything we can do for them, so we try to point them in the right direction. Over the years, we've developed a great list of resources for people to get the help they need, even if it's not related to our law firm.

If the consultation is set and the person (or the person's family) meets with me, I'll have all of the notes from the initial conversations with my staff; the staff will have already informed them about the items they should ideally bring to the meeting. After reviewing those items, I ask them what they would like to accomplish, and then listen to their needs, concerns, and goals; then I tell them the available solutions.

Depending on the type of legal matter, each type would involve a different set of necessary items or pieces of information; all of these items are outlined. For example, on a long-term care planning case involving a stay in a nursing home, the client will want to have some financial security. We'll need to know the income, assets, veteran status (including discharge papers), and all of the estate planning documents currently in place.

MY FOUR AREAS OF PRACTICE

My practice deals with four primary areas: long-term care planning and public benefits, guardianship, estate planning, and estate administration. Long-term care planning helps people who are worried about their own or their loved one's stay in a nursing home. In this area of law, it's helpful that we have knowledge of Medicaid, Medicare, Social Security, and Veterans benefits, as well as other resources within the community. We also help people obtain Social Security Disability benefits.

Some people arrive at our office in crisis mode, because their loved one has already been admitted for a long hospital stay or into a rehabilitation facility, and sometimes the loved one is not coming home. If they learn that Medicare will not pay for the custodial stay, most people can't afford the cost of care in Nevada, which averages $7,000 per month. (This amount varies across the country.) If the family can't afford much, they look at what they can do to protect the assets without spending every dime.

Secondly, I handle guardianships. In other states, this area is called "conservatorship." It deals with people who did not plan ahead before becoming incapacitated, who cannot manage their affairs independently and require outside help. In these cases, the attorney petitions for guardianship, so that the person appointed as a guardian can legally help the person who has diminished capacity.

Most people can avoid guardianships by planning ahead, putting good documents in place, and naming good decision makers; our office can help with these things via estate planning. However, many times, our office sees exploitation – someone is taking advantage of the vulnerable person whose capacity is beginning to slide into decline. If the family member becomes concerned about someone taking advantage, if appropriate, we can petition for guardianship.

In traditional estate planning, we assist the client to get affairs in order prior to incapacitation or death. The client doesn't necessarily need to have an appointed guardian. Our estate planning often focuses upon long-term care planning. We customize the documents to address the concerns most often encountered by those who become incapacitated.

Legally, the age of the person does not matter for estate planning; a person in their twenties or thirties can visit an attorney to put together a will, trust, or various powers of attorney. We do planning for families of all ages. For instance, families with minor children should consider having a trust set up for the minor children. Most people don't get their finances and documents in order until they get older, or until a spouse is diagnosed with a disease like Alzheimer's, but there are no legal barriers to setting up an estate plan or a trust.

The fourth and final area includes estate administration, for both probates and trusts. If someone dies, there are legal steps that should be taken, so that everything from proper notices to handling of debts and taxes is done correctly. It helps to have a good qualified attorney assisting you during that process.

OUR PHILOSOPHY OF SUCCESS

My work focuses on doing the right thing. I do what is best for the client, and as a result, over the years, I have developed a reputation for doing what's best. People feel that they can trust me because I will tell them what they have to do, and what they don't need to do. Sometimes I tell them that they don't need to make any changes in what they're doing, or I'll offer them lower-cost alternatives.

As an attorney, I take a good look at the objective. I see what the client wants to accomplish, and then think of ways to accomplish those goals in a way that will cause the least number of negative ripples. I think about how the client will feel about the goals and the process, and decide whether or not we can accomplish those objectives without adding any additional stress or harm to others involved.

As an attorney, it's important to discern what your client wants, and then determine the best way to get there. Find good mentors, good teachers, and read good books, then put together your plan and stick with it. I recommend this classic book: *Think and Grow Rich*. I also love the book: *The One Thing* by Gary Keller. I have followed his daily action plan and it has been great for my quality of life.

I have always loved to read, and I love to incorporate what I learn from books into my own life. I think that's another part of success. Don't just learn - take what you have learned and actually apply it to the business of living.

(This content should be used for informational purposes only. It does not create an attorney-client relationship with any reader and should not be construed as legal advice. If you need legal advice, please contact an attorney in your community who can assess the specifics of your situation.)

6

ONE OF THE
SMART ONES

by Matthew Meyer, Esq.

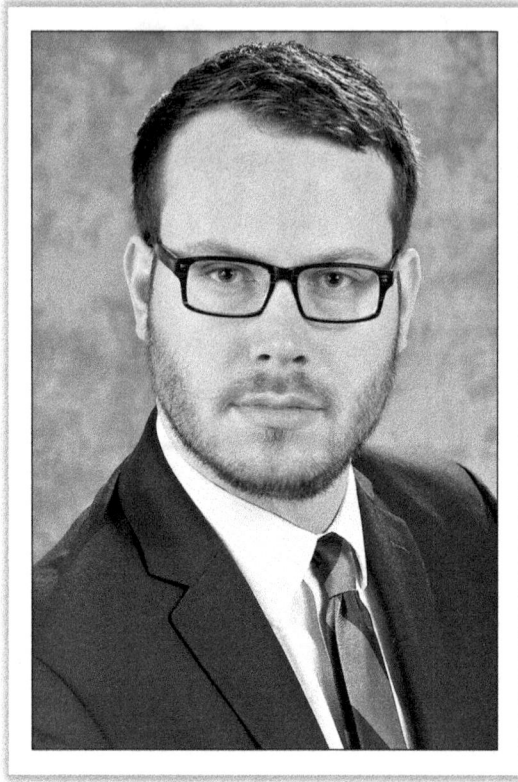

Matthew Meyer, Esq.
Meyer Van Severen, SC
Milwaukee, Wisconsin
www.mvslegal.com

Matthew Meyer is a Milwaukee criminal defense attorney who dedicates his practice to defending the constitutional rights of those accused of violating the laws of the State of Wisconsin and the United States of America.

Attorney Meyer received his Bachelor of Arts from the University of Wisconsin-Madison in 2008 as a political science major. He received his Juris Doctorate from Marquette University Law School in 2012, where he was actively involved in the Marquette Volunteer Legal Clinic and the Marquette University Small Claims Mediation Clinic. During his final year of law school Meyer interned with the Wisconsin State Public Defender Trial Office.

In October 2014 Matthew Meyer founded Meyer Law Office. The following year he joined Benjamin Van Severen and formed Meyer Van Severen, S.C.

Attorney Meyer has received numerous awards throughout his career, including being named by the National Trial Lawyers to the Top 100 Trial Lawyers and Top 40 under 40 Trial Lawyers in Wisconsin. Meyer was most recently recognized by the American Institute of Criminal Law Attorneys as a top 10 Best Criminal Law Attorney for Client Satisfaction. In 2015 Meyer was once again nominated for these awards. Additionally, he was nominated by M Magazine as a 2015 Leading Lawyer in criminal defense. Super Lawyers first recognized Meyer as a "Rising Star" in 2015. Meyer maintains a 10/10 "superb" rating on avvo.com.

ONE OF THE SMART ONES

WISCONSIN ROOTS

I grew up in Wausau, Wisconsin, a small town right in the middle of the state. I'd describe my family as blue collar which is to say, my mom is a nurse and my dad works in a paper factory. Growing up, my parents often pointed out to me that as much as I enjoyed arguing, I'd be a natural lawyer. I hadn't really considered such a career until the day I was standing with my grandma—my dad's mother—in her kitchen on her farm. We were talking about doctors and lawyers when she said, "Matt, doctors and lawyers are the smart ones." That stuck with me.

One of the things in life that always motivates me is when someone suggests that I might not be able to do something. Whether she meant it as a challenge or not, to me it seemed that my grandma had just been told me that I couldn't possibly be smart enough to achieve such a career goal. So, from that moment forward, I knew I had to become a lawyer.

Reading was difficult for me. I learned to read a grade or two later than a lot of my peers, and I still remember the struggle. It was certainly one of the most difficult and frustrating tasks I ever took on. Looking back, I think the problem was that I was basically a lazy kid when it came to my early education. Being outside and doing my own thing was far more important than studying. I didn't want to sit around reading books. I had better things to do. Eventually, though, I realized that people thought I was stupid and not bright enough to keep up with the others. It was that realization that hooked the fighter in me. (Cue the Rocky theme.) "I can do this. I'm going to figure this out." And so, I did.

To this day, I use this same strategy to handle each and every challenge that comes along in my life. When I'm faced with any kind of battle; first I own it, and then I say, "Hey, this is the problem. This is the way I want to fix it, and this is how I'm going to do it." The most powerful motivators, for me at least, is when someone tells me I can't do something.

I lived in Wausau until I was 19 then attended the University of Wisconsin in Madison, Wisconsin. I earned my Bachelor of Arts degree in political science there. Subsequently, I started law school at a small college in Miami, Florida. Later, I transferred to back to Wisconsin where I received my law degree from Marquette University in Milwaukee.

Marquette does a great job offering internships and other opportunities for law students to learn about all aspects of law. My first internship was a mediation clinic, where we helped people with small claims issues. (In this case "small claims" referred to anything under $10,000.) Whenever anybody would sue someone else, one of the first steps was to learn if the parties wanted to mediate, or try to come to a mutually agreeable resolution. As a student I would lead the mediation and try to reach a point in negotiations that worked for all the parties involved. It was a great experience since it allowed me to work with people who were on opposite sides of an issue.

It was intimidating at first, but it was a valuable experience that allowed me to get involved in the court system even though I was still in law school. During my final year of law school, I interned with the Wisconsin State Public Defender Trial Office. That was another great experience because, even as a law student, I was able to appear on the record and argue cases as an attorney. I didn't do any trials, but I had the opportunity to do motion arguments and be involved in the sentencing phase of the process. The experience offered me the opportunity to perform the research and writing, as well affording me experience on the procedural side of law. Of course, focusing on what's in the books is important, but there's no substitute for hands-on experience. That OJT was helpful as I started my own career and my own firm, because there are little procedural points that you don't always learn about in law school. Professors can't go over every last thing. In court there are certain points where you need to do things or say things that aren't covered in school, and the internship helped fill in those blanks.

I decided to stay in Milwaukee because it's the only city in Wisconsin large enough where it's financially feasible to focus entirely on criminal defense. Criminal law is more difficult in smaller communities, because in order to keep the firm afloat, you've got to specialize in something else. In those communities you're often forced to do general practice, or split your time working in other areas. I didn't want to do that. I wanted to do criminal defense and drunk driving work exclusively.

THE ROMANCE OF CRIMINAL LAW

I decided that I wanted to do criminal law because it has always interested me and by its very nature, always provides a challenge. I think there's something romantic and heroic about standing beside and defending a person against the full force of the government. I mean, you literally have the county you're in, the state of Wisconsin, or even the United States squaring off against your client, and sometimes you're the only person the accused has to rely upon. I feel passionately about the Constitution and making sure we defend and uphold the principles there. In this nation, the Constitution requires us to make sure that each and all—even those who we might define as the worst of the worst—receive the same protections under the law.

Along those lines, people always ask me, "How can you defend bad people?" First of all, I don't consider whether a person is bad or good. You can't look at it that way. You've got to understand that each of us deserves a defense. We are all innocent until the government proves us to be guilty. No case can be over or settled until due process is satisfied. We're all guaranteed that, and that doesn't go away no matter how scary the government's allegations are.

Even the weakest, poorest, least civilized people in society must be afforded the same rights and the same protection as those who are seen as the "best." As soon as you allow any erosion of those Constitutional rights and protections from the people on the bottom, that misuse of the law inevitably works its way up to Joe Average. So it's a slippery slope, and it's something we need to watch out for. Lawyers are the vanguard in the line of defense against an encroaching government.

DWI CAN HAPPEN TO ANYBODY

You'd be surprised at how many people who get a first or second offense are otherwise responsible people. In most of my first, second, or third offense cases, the people involved generally have no other criminal background. They're people who simply had a few too many drinks. They're just a few points above where they need to be. They attended a dinner or holiday party, and then suddenly they're being arrested along the side of the road and taken away to sit in jail for at least a few hours. These people aren't always habitual drunks. Each of us (unless someone doesn't drink at all,) might do something social—have dinner, go to a party, and have a few drinks—and suddenly we can find ourselves in handcuffs. So these aren't the people who are out shooting each other or committing armed robberies. They're simply the ones who made a poor choice.

In Wisconsin, drunk driving is generally charged as an OWI, which stands for "Operating While Intoxicated." The way the statute is written, it allows prosecutors to charge either OWI or DWI, which is "Driving While Intoxicated."

Operating is a broader term. Obviously, "driving" means moving, steering, and manipulating the vehicle, but "operating" can also mean that you've done something that allows you to operate the vehicle, such as putting the key in the ignition and turning the car on. Sitting in your car without the keys in the ignition isn't enough to be actually "operating" that vehicle. You must manipulate the controls putting the vehicle in a position wherein it can be driven. You can also be charged with OWI for using vehicles other than an actual car. The statute says, "Incapable of safely driving." And the statute begins with "No person may drive or operate a motor vehicle..." Motor vehicle means "a vehicle ... which is self-propelled... except a vehicle operated exclusively on rail." So it can includes tractors, snowmobiles, boats, motorcycles, and other motorized vehicles.

You also hear about PAC in Wisconsin, which stands for "Prohibited Alcohol Concentration." It is a charge that very commonly comes along with an OWI charge. The PAC reflects the level of alcohol in the bloodstream considered to be illegal. Here, .08 is the prohibited number for your first offense. Even if you're driving safely, if you're pulled over and your blood alcohol level is found to be above .08, you can be charged with PAC. An OWI charge doesn't deal with that .08 prohibition; it means that you're intoxicated to the extent that you can't operate the vehicle, regardless of your blood alcohol content. Often when an OWI/PAC case is pled, the PAC charge is dismissed and judgment is entered on the OWI.

Technically speaking, a DUI is not a driving offense in Wisconsin. In other states, there are driving offenses under that name, but not here. However, as a practical matter, some of our marketing actually focuses on the term "DUI" since that particular term is used in most other states. When you come to Wisconsin from another state and get a drunken driving ticket, what are you going to look up? You will very likely going look up "DUI," because it is the term with which you are most familiar.

BEYOND HANGING OUT YOUR SHINGLE

Advertising and having an online presence is very important for a law firm. If you get in trouble, what are you going to do? The first thing you're going to do is go online and search for the best criminal defense attorney you can afford. So, one of the first things I did when I launched my firm was make sure I had an online presence. I wanted to make sure my firm appeared if someone searched for important keywords like "Milwaukee criminal lawyer" or even longer-tail search terms like "who is the best Milwaukee criminal defense attorney."

The first step was buying a powerful domain name. We're currently registered as milwaukee-criminal-lawyer.com. I couldn't believe that was still available when we purchased it, because it carries so much power in and of itself. In starting my law firm, I worked a couple 100-hour weeks during my first three months just writing articles, describing crimes, and writing about how to deal with this or how to deal with that. That's another example of me owning the problem, jumping in, and figuring it out. I could have hired someone to write those articles for me, but I think there's great value in learning and understanding basic online marketing and search engine optimization principles. I thought, "Which is better; a lawyer who knows what he's talking about and can throw in the relevant search terms and the key phrases, or some guy out there who's a pro with search engine optimization but doesn't know anything about the law itself?"

I didn't know anything about SEO or online marketing before starting my own firm, so I went on a self-guided crash course by reading articles online. Even now, I keep up-to-date on the best practices for enhancing online search results for my firm. Somehow, I beat the other firms for the Google rankings, and many of them have dedicated SEO people and marketing professionals. I've come up as one of the top responses pretty consistently for very important Google search terms. You don't have to have official training to make yourself visible online. All I use is Google Analytics, Google Webmaster Tools, and a simple SEO plug-in on my website. I'm in a smaller market, but even so, I was top-ranked on Google before I even rented an office. I was operating my firm from a 13-inch laptop in my one-bedroom apartment, meeting clients at coffee shops, and working on the volume.

When I brought Benjamin Van Severen on as a partner, I told him, "Ben, you need to write 56 blog posts over the next year, one a week, and those blog terms must be SEO solid. That's going to be the most important thing you can do for both of us." That was one of the things that I really focused on in our negotiations starting up Meyer Van Severen, S.C., because internet presence is the most important thing for our future. It wasn't a short term, "Hey, I'm going to pay you a couple thousand dollars to join on." It's not about the up-front money, because if Ben writes 56 blog posts and each one of those gets us ranked for some long-tail keyword, then that's actually much more powerful than a short term bit of money could ever be.

Aside from searches, one of the places that clients find attorneys is through online directories. There are a number of directory services for lawyers: Avvo.com, FindLaw.com, and Lawyers.com are some popular ones. As the potential client searches, one or more of those services will come up near the top of the search results, and the potential client will be directed back to your firm. You have to pay to show up on most of those directories, but if a few potential clients find your firm, it's worth the fee. We see these things like real estate. If my website, Avvo, and Findlaw are three of the top four results, there's a 75% chance you'll end up looking at my firm. But if it's just my website, the chances you'll see me are pretty slim.

That's the difference I see between a lot of older attorneys, who are purely relying on word of mouth to spread the word about their services, and the newer attorneys, who are really doing it right. As far as I can tell, I was the first attorney in Milwaukee, or within our region, who actually had conversations with his clients about writing online reviews. Eventually, I got enough reviews for Google to give me a five-star rating, which pushed me to the top of the map results where everyone could see me, and that, in turn, allowed me to continue to sign up new clients, do good work, and receive more positive reviews. So, getting client reviews, appearing in paid advertising directories, and having a good website, all allow for search terms to direct back to you. This is important in today's legal environment, because the world we practice in is not what it was 10, 15, 20 years ago. You must market online these days, and that has made my focus a little different. I haven't focused so much on the networking itself, although with any career you must do some networking. I have focused on working hard and having those results speak for themselves. Word spreads, and so that really gets me to the same point as networking, just by a different route.

There are certain websites where you can pay to achieve a certain score. I believe that's a disservice to the client. On the other hand, when you get 10.0 on Avvo, it really means something. You can't just write a check and make a perfect score appear; you have to work to achieve it. To build your score, you have to get awards, some work under your belt, and have other attorneys endorse you. I think Avvo is the one company that is the most important, as far as client referrals and online presence, because they are often number one or number two for those long-tail search terms that people use when they search. And you must have a 10.0. If you don't have a 10.0, what is the potential client going to do? She's going to go to the guys with a 10.0. If you've got a 9.8 or 9.7, she's going to say, "Hey, what's wrong with this attorney? I've got 15 other guys here with a rating of 10.0, and I can go with any of them."

Once you have the Internet saturated, you can turn back to more personal advertising. You can add in the real-life things that people see wherever they turn, like billboards and electronic boards, to build name recognition. My firm is currently doing this. We're advertising on screens in the Bradley Center, which is where the Milwaukee Bucks play. We're also advertising on screens located in bars, because that's often where people are before picking up a drunk driving charge. Then, when something does happen, they can say, "Hey, what was that guy's name I saw in the bathroom the other day at the bar? Oh, it's Matt Meyer. Maybe he can help me with this drunk driving ticket." If the potential client can remember my name, then all it takes is a quick Google search to pull up my contact info and give me a call.

I think some of the hesitancy to use Internet advertising is a generational thing. My generation grew up with the Internet. We're comfortable with it. It's second nature to use it. A lot of our clients are going to be in the same age group, so it makes sense to list ourselves on the Internet so they can find us. A lot of the older generations are worried about being ripped off, and it's possible. I get calls every single week from somebody trying to sell some directory listing or service I don't need. I made that mistake as a young attorney. I spent $3,000.00 for a service, and didn't see any results. It was frustrating, but with some research and conversations with tech-savvy attorneys, it was pretty easy to figure out where to go. There's always going to be lessons, bumps, and bruises. It can be difficult finding out which resources are legitimate and respectable online. You have to fail sometimes; the important thing is to make sure those failures aren't too drastic. In short, I think today's attorneys should be embracing technology, embracing the Internet, and embracing the way people find clients in this technical age.

GOOD LAWYERS LISTEN

I think that the key to being a great lawyer is staying down to earth and connecting with your client on a very basic level. One of the best ways to do that is listening to your clients. You must spend whatever time it takes to understand what your client is saying, and to figure out exactly what the issue is. I think that if you don't spend that time listening to the story, you really don't have a chance. I consistently hear from my clients, "Hey, I called this old guy and he was rude." If your clients don't feel valued by you, they will move on to the next attorney without hesitation.

Listening, learning, and understanding the problem is part and parcel of being a good lawyer, but it's also the meat of running a good business. I worked at Starbucks for seven years throughout the end of high school and into college. That business really focuses on taking care of the client or the customer. If you're charging five bucks for a cup of coffee, depending on where you are, who's going to pay for it if you're mean to them? It was a great learning experience.

I think that taking time to connect with clients is where a lot of other attorneys falter. They either quote a fee too quickly or say,

"Hey, this is what it's going to cost," and don't listen to the entire story. I've spent a half hour to 45 minutes on the phone with somebody only to find that they either won't pay or don't have the ability to pay a fee, or something else doesn't work out. It's frustrating when you spend an hour on the phone with a potential client and he doesn't call you back or he's just milking you for information. But those people aren't where we need to focus. The focus should be on making sure your clients know you're there to help them. You establish that fact in the very beginning. I think if I quote you a fee within five minutes of talking to you, it shows you that this is just about the money; it's not about taking care of you as a person.

Additionally, I give clients a cell phone number where they can call me, and they can text me. Texting is a big deal for clients because they like the ability to be able to reach out to the attorney whenever they have a question or concern. My policy has always been to call clients back by the end of the day. Make sure that you respond to them and that they know you're still in their corner, on their team, and still working on their case. They develop a trust that they've got this connection with you. Ultimately, I believe being a great lawyer is all about treating people well, doing good work, and working hard for clients.

Even though I'm one the youngest guys charging reasonable fees, there's always somebody that's going to be cheaper. Frankly, I think cheaper often means you get less hard work. It's bargain basement representation. My first boss's philosophy was charge high fees and work for them. If I charge you an appropriate fee, I'm going to work hard for that fee. If I only charge you $2,000 to work on a felony case that's going to go trial, it doesn't make sense compared to the number of hours I'm going to put in.

I'm concerned when I hear about people who shop for the cheapest attorney in town. The question is, will that lawyer answer your text message? Will he or she give you a cell phone number, or respond on the weekends or after business hours? I think that wraps back into taking care of the person and being down to earth. We're not the cheapest lawyers. A lot of people say that my firm is expensive, but it's all about working for you and your outcome. In order to do that, it has to make sense for you, and it has to make sense for me - not only as a lawyer but also a man running a business.

YOUTH AND ENTHUSIASM VS. OLD AGE AND EXPERIENCE

One of the obstacles that my partner Ben and I face in business is that we are certainly the young guys in town doing what we do. I am 30 years old. I don't have any gray hairs, and the hair I have hasn't really started falling out yet. I am not married and don't have kids, so I've really focused the past couple years of my life on this career. It's tough because people often want to hire the old guys. Some folks just don't want to hire the young guns. It's reasonable that they have some misgivings. They think, "Hey, this guy just got of law school in 2012; he hasn't been doing this all that long. Why would I hire him as opposed to somebody who's been doing it 20, 25, or 30 years?"

What we've done to counter this is focus on the smart, serious representation. Every single criminal defense lawyer you're going to find who is marketing his services will call himself aggressive. That's cliché. It's outdated, so we don't use that word. What we're trying to do is brand our firm as the young, smart guys in town. Since we're the closest to our university days, we're the guys with the 'freshest' information on the statutes; we'll work longer hours, and also answer your text messages.

The Evolving Legal Landscape

The prosecutorial atmosphere is changing, too. Milwaukee experienced a very violent year in 2015. You've got DAs and prosecutors who are coming down harder on certain crimes. You've got a heroin epidemic in the area, too, and people dying from it. So depending upon the kind of case you're working on, and the level of press coverage involved, plea offers seemed to ratchet up a bit recently.

Certain prosecutors want to lock people up. They don't focus on rehabilitation, which is what it will take ultimately to bring these crime rates down. There are so many pieces that intertwine. Even before rehabilitation, we should focus on figuring out a way to reach people, especially in the rougher areas of our communities, before they contribute to the problem. When you have a client who robbed somebody or is selling heroin, the state throws out some crazy prison recommendation and wants to send your client away for 20 years. Just Friday, I had a client sent to prison for 18 years based upon a couple of armed robberies. The frustration there is that I don't think locking these individuals up for a quarter of their lives is the way to fix this. I spoke to the DA about that case on Friday and I said, "Hey, how do we fix this? What do we do? There's got to be something other than sending young males, often young black males, to prison. What do we do?" How do we do that? I don't know, and I don't think there's just one easy answer, but it's something we need to figure out.

Politics also comes into play with that. It's that whole "tough on crime" thing, which, unfortunately, works for those who are running for office. Are you going to vote for the guy who says, "I send bad people to prison," or are you going to vote for the guy who says, "I send bad people down the street to the psychologist to see what's going on under the hood?" It's easy to say, "Hey, that's scary. I don't want that guy down the street from me. I want that guy locked up. I want him behind razor wire where he can never touch me." I think that politics plays an interesting role because the rehabilitation approach doesn't get the votes. The guys that are tough on crime get the votes.

I do think we're making some small, slow progress. I think the probes in the police departments across the country and more oversight by the federal government will ultimately make a difference. Recently, Milwaukee brought in a bunch of body cameras that the police officers wear on their uniforms. A few days after the rollout, there was a hostage situation, and the events were recorded on the police officer's body camera. The hostage taker ended up shooting himself, but the two hostages were safe. The cameras seemed to show officers following protocol, and were not involved negatively in the death. Although ballistics would have figured this out, the video made this easier for the public to understand.

On the flip side of that, the frustration that we have in Milwaukee is that the cameras can be turned off and on. The police response to that is sometimes it's important to be able to turn off the camera in a domestic violence situation or sexual assault situation where the privacy of the victim is very important. The issue I have is that if you have the ability to turn off the camera, then if you know you're going to do something bad, you could just turn that camera off. I'm not sure of all the procedural elements, and I'm sure there will be some kinks to work out and some trial and error needed, I think the cameras will aid the legal system at the end of the day.

I think that as long as we continue to develop more transparency, things will get better.

But as long as we have the problem of crime in this country, we will still have to determine guilt or innocence. That brings me back to why I wanted to become a criminal defense lawyer in the first place. It's one of the questions that friends and family always ask. As I mentioned earlier, everybody always wants to know, "How can you defend someone if you know they're guilty?" I've even had people say, "There must be something wrong with you, Matt, if you're able to do that." I have to decide how to explain this clearly to someone who might be thinking on an emotional level and not understanding the bigger picture. I have to explain that it doesn't matter if the accused is guilty or innocent because, either way, the government still has its job to do.

Sometimes citizens forget that. It's never our job as citizens to prove ourselves innocent, although it might sometimes seem that way. The government's job is to prove us guilty. It doesn't matter to me if a client is guilty or innocent because I'm going to do the same work, and that is to make sure the government does its job. I'm going to put the government through the same steps to make them prove their case. Getting to the guilt or innocence doesn't change what my job is. And I don't think that it's really all that important—it's not my job to find them guilty or to find them innocent. It's my job to make sure that the government does its job and that my client's constitutional rights are protected.

It's really easy in this litigious society for somebody to falsely accuse you of something. Before you know it, you're picked up and taken in for questioning, and that brings me back to the comment I made earlier about shopping for the cheapest attorney in town. When you're accused of a crime, you want to get a successful attorney to defend you. You need somebody whom you know is going to do well for you; who has client reviews, has independent sources out there saying positive things, because now you're talking about consequences that affect the rest of your life. Once you're accused of committing a crime, there are only a few steps until you could be convicted of committing that crime. And unfortunately, a criminal conviction – including charges related to alcohol and driving - is something that will follow you for the rest of your life and can impact your ability to earn a living, buy a house, or even find a significant other. A conviction is a serious, life-altering thing.

I don't think there's a more valuable investment that individuals accused of a crime can make than making sure that they have hired a good attorney. They need the attorney who, along with doing good work, will call and text them back. They don't want an attorney whose main interest is keeping his involvement in the case in tune time-wise with the price quote he made in the beginning. You want an attorney who can make the cloud go away, or at least make it where you can point to it and say, "I was found innocent, thank you very much."

I believe that older attorneys have all kinds of advantages, but that doesn't mean we younger guys don't have some edges of our own. We're hungrier. We have the edge of being eager to prove ourselves. We're putting everything we have into it because we have everything to win, not just for the client, but also for ourselves. So we're ultra-committed and we have a bunch of youthful enthusiasm that can trump old age and acumen in the long run.

(This content should be used for informational purposes only. It does not create an attorney-client relationship with any reader and should not be construed as legal advice. If you need legal advice, please contact an attorney in your community who can assess the specifics of your situation.)

7

—

A Creative Perspective: A Lawyer Who Thinks Outside The Box

by Laurie B. Gengo, Esq.

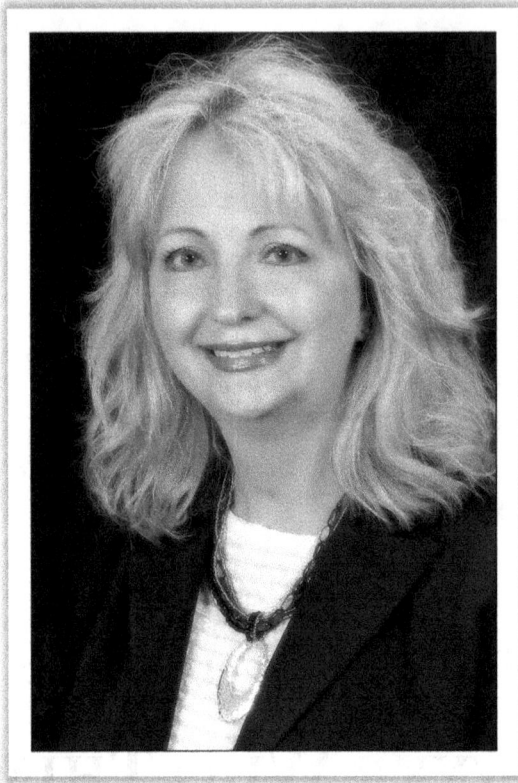

Laurie B. Gengo, Esq.
Triangle Law Group
Raleigh, North Carolina
www.trianglelawgroup.net

Laurie B. Gengo is the founder and owner of Triangle Law Group ("TLG"), a small boutique law-firm based in Raleigh, North Carolina.

Ms. Gengo is a native of Jamestown, New York, and received her Bachelor of Art Summa Cum Laude from the State University of New York at Geneseo in 1980. She earned her law degree from the State University of New York at Buffalo in 1985 where she also was a Ph.D student in Political Science, and served as an Instructor for the 1985-1986 academic year. Laurie is also a licensed real estate broker in the State of North Carolina and the owner of Trilogy Real Estate Group, LLC, and a co-owner of several real estate investment LLC's.

She is admitted to the state bar in Indiana and North Carolina and may practice before the United States District Court for the Eastern and Western Districts of North Carolina.

A CREATIVE PERSPECTIVE: A LAWYER WHO THINKS OUTSIDE THE BOX

GROWING UP IN JAMESTOWN

I grew up in Jamestown, which is located in western New York. Even though it is a small town with only about 30,000 people, it was a mecca for creative people. Lucille Ball was born there, giving the town a reason to open a very interesting museum, the Lucille Ball-Desi Arnaz Center, in our little downtown. Supreme Court Justice Robert Jackson grew up in Frewsburg, a town very close to Jamestown, and practiced law in Jamestown for a period of time. Most of the original band members of the 10,000 Maniacs band also grew up in Jamestown. They have made several platinum records and have been a cornerstone of alternative rock. In addition, Roger Tory Peterson (known for multiple reasons as an artist) was from Jamestown.

Jamestown is a very pretty place near the Chautauqua Institution, which is a Victorian community on a lake that is very dedicated to the visual and performing arts. It has an opera house and it continues training new musical professionals. The institution brings in speakers and performers from all over the world. Growing up in that type of area gave me a good foundation for where I am today.

Both of my parents were born and raised in Jamestown, where they raised my sister and me. My mom was born in the United States; both of my mom's parents were from Sweden and my dad's father was from Sweden. His mother was born in nearby Pennsylvania, but grew up in Jamestown. In the past, it was a town inhabited primarily by Scandinavian and Italian people; they had relocated for work because the area was once the furniture capital of the United States, similar to High Point, North Carolina today.

Jamestown, like many northern towns, suffered an economic decline. However, it has recently undergone a well-deserved renaissance. When you grow up in such a unique place, you are fortunate to be surrounded by people from other countries and different cultures. I loved growing up there, surrounded by great food and great ethnic grocery stores where you could buy cheese and spaghetti sauce from Italy. Today, you can buy these specialty items on the Internet or almost anywhere, but the choices were limited back then. We were able to experience a lot that most small-town people wouldn't have been exposed to even though Jamestown is a rural and mountainous area. Many areas like Jamestown can be very isolated.

I loved going to Chautauqua growing up. By having the lake and Chautauqua nearby, it made Jamestown a special and beautiful place to grow up. I played the flute, so I was able to attend the Institution on scholarships that allowed me take lessons from musical professionals over the summer. For about five or six years, I was allowed to train with many professionals. My parents are still in Jamestown, so when I go visit, I still go up to Chautauqua to take in a concert, a book reading, or an opera.

MY SCHOOL YEARS IN JAMESTOWN

The three junior high schools spanned the seventh, eighth, and ninth grades. Going to Jefferson Junior High School was a fun time in my life; we recently had a junior high reunion after nearly 40 years. After junior high, all three schools funnel students into the one and only high school in our town, Jamestown High School. It is the first time that students from all three schools come together; for some, it was the first time they had met each other.

In high school, I kept very busy playing the flute in the marching band. It was fun for me to watch all of the football games, both home and away games, and be part of a sorority. High school itself wasn't all fun, though. In my senior year, my dad was diagnosed with throat cancer caused from smoking. He survived surgery but he was unable to come to my graduation. Up to that point, everything had been moving in the right direction but that event put a damper on everything. Thankfully, he is still around today, living in the very house that I grew up in so the story has a great ending!

My college years started at Jamestown Community College. I transferred into the system of the State University of New York, specifically the campus in Geneseo (SUNY Geneseo) where I received my Bachelor's Degree in Political Science with a Minor in Criminal Justice. Unlike most people who have the luxury of treating college as a social experience, I spent all of my time studying because I knew that I wanted to go on to law school and I knew how competitive that would be for me. I was determined to reach my goals, and did not want anything to get in my way!

Next, I attended the State University of New York at Buffalo, School of Law, where I earned my law degree. Buffalo was similar to Jamestown, only much bigger and very cold with a lot of snow. Though it was beautiful, I was still focused on my education; therefore, I didn't spend much of my time enjoying it. I just knew what I wanted and remained focus on getting my law degree.

FORMIDABLE FORCES

At 17 years old, finding out that my dad had cancer put an entirely new spin on life for me. It showed me that, as a woman, I needed to move forward and decide what I wanted to do with my life. Of course, there was a time when I wondered whether my dad would live or not and, if the treatment didn't work, how would all of us be able to survive? My mom worked but my dad had the larger income in our family.

His cancer made me realize that our lives are very precious and that our lives can change at a moment's notice. That translated into why I am where I am today. I no longer become stressed out over the small things as I did when I was younger. My dad being diagnosed with cancer made me realize that no one is guaranteed tomorrow so we need to enjoy what we have today and use our skills in the best way possible to be able to take care of ourselves and become independent.

There is so much that I don't remember from that time, probably because I blocked it out of my mind, but I do remember him in the hospital and the moment when we learned that he had cancer. I also remember him writing me a letter telling me he was sorry he couldn't attend my graduation in Chautauqua. That time of my life was scary; I didn't know for sure that he was going to be all right, and neither did he.

CHOOSING A CREATIVE CAREER

I always wanted to work in a field that would allow me to utilize my creativity. Maybe some people will laugh at this, but in my mind, I thought the legal field would be perfect for utilizing my creativity. I excelled at art when a young child, and still create my own artistic "masterpieces" today in my home art studio. I felt the legal field would provide me with another outlet for my creativity. Today, people watch television shows about the legal system and, honestly, it does not depict real life. I thought the legal field would give me the opportunity to develop different legal arguments and interpretations that would be considered creative.

Truthfully, if I had been able to do what I originally wanted to do, I would have been a veterinarian because I love animals. In fact, I spent a summer with a veterinarian just to see if I really liked veterinary work as much as I thought I did. After seeing people losing the pets they considered part of their family, I decided that the veterinary field just wasn't for me – I couldn't handle the sadness of it. Even though I didn't become a veterinarian, I still love to be around animals. My husband and I have been married for almost eight years now but we've never had any children. My husband's son, who is 27, lives with us while he is working toward earning his MBA and he has a dog. Along with our rescued dog and cat, and my stepson's rescued ninety pound dog, we have a bit of a fun, little zoo right now.

After the summer with the veterinarian, I got even more focused about attending law school. Soon I realized there weren't very many women in the legal field — nowhere near the number of male lawyers. Most women were paralegals, not lawyers. I have always enjoyed a challenge, so I decided then and there that I was going to law school, though I had no idea how to pay for it.

I didn't let obstacles stop me from reaching my goals because I had decided to do it one way or another. It would have been easy for me to give in to the difficulties and just stay a small-town girl, but I didn't do that – even though I still love where I'm grew up. When I retire, I still want to live in Jamestown part-time because I still have so many good friends there. And, I really love Chautauqua and the lake!

THE ARTS AND EXPRESSION

Besides my dad and his cancer, another big influence was my love of music and my parents' encouragement to play an instrument. That encouragement allowed me to receive the scholarships I did to take lessons at Chautauqua free of charge.

One of my best friends still lives in the Chautauqua area, and even though I hardly ever see her now, we still have a great relationship. She is very artistic and we created a long-term plan in our early years to begin some sort of art "thing" together. We haven't decided exactly where it will be located; however, it will be in the Jamestown/Chautauqua area. As we grew older, we went our separate ways. Because we are so close, I anticipate we will gravitate back to where we started, as so many others do as they grow older. I suspect we will have some type of art gallery in the distant future where we will display and sell our artistic creations.

Usually, I think of influences as people who have had an impact on my life, rather than events that have happened. If I had to pick an event, though, it would have to be my dad's illness.

MY PHILOSOPHY FOR SUCCESS

I believe if you try hard enough and you are determined enough, you can reach any goal you set for yourself. I believe having a positive attitude has a great influence on your life. Growing up, I was not the most positive person but through practicing music and visual art, the creativity taught me patience. My philosophy would be that you can do anything that you want if you put your mind to it and don't let the negativity drag you down.

I realize that not everyone shares my perspective. Sometimes people are in a bad mood and when you say something like that to them, you sound like a "peppy Pollyanna" but I still believe it's true. If you try hard enough and believe you can be a success, then you will be successful. If you convince yourself that you are or will be a disaster, it becomes a self-fulfilling prophecy so you become the disaster. I don't know if you ever studied psychology in school but if you convince yourself that you are a failure or that you will never succeed in anything, you'll psychologically cause that result. On the other hand, if you view things as a "yes" — "Yes, I can do that, I can make it work," then you will make it work.

Neither of my parents graduated from college but my sister and I both earned our law degrees. She is an attorney in South Carolina and I think it's because we both shared the ambition and the determination of our parents and that we grew up in a very special small town.

THE FUTURE OF MY PROFESSION

One of the things that bothers me — it is really popular in North Carolina — are the companies that offer "canned" legal documents. These internet-based companies sell wills and other legal documents to people at a low cost so the consumer "saves" money. The documents are often not drafted well nor do they comply with North Carolina law. As I see it, companies like this are trying to take over the practice of law. Personally, I don't think they ever will succeed long term, but the economy has forced people to use the service they can afford, even if that service is not the best option. I am hopeful that the economy will get better. People will then realize that if you are in the legal field and you provide excellent service at an affordable price, our profession will continue to grow. And, they will also realize that you get what you pay for.

One of the biggest changes I have seen in my profession is the move toward electronic books. For example, you can access statutes on your computer instead of using a physical book. Even though the electronic world is making the way we receive information faster and easier, I'm "old school" so I believe you need to have the real thing in front of you. A computer document or book makes you dependent on the Internet working. If the Internet goes down, you need to have the real thing in front of you.

I do think that my profession is moving in the right direction and people are beginning to understand the importance of lawyers and understand that legal services can be very affordable. The large, more expensive law firms are beginning to disappear. They are being replaced with smaller, more affordable law practices. I began my legal career with a large firm before I went through the cycle of working for smaller and smaller law firms until I began my own law practice. Now, people who couldn't afford to pay the fees large firms charge clients to fight for them are finding it easier to find an affordable lawyer.

I would love to see more women start their own business, not necessarily just in the law field but in any field. I have given seminars on this subject. This past April, I sponsored a seminar at an annual conference called Women's Empowerment, held at the PNC arena where the Carolina Hurricanes play. The conference was organized and promoted by a local radio station. The seminar covered how to start and run your own business and the conference was only open to women. With more than 250 women, and standing room only, there was so much positive energy in the room. After the 90-minute seminar, the other business owners and I conducted a panel discussion. It was a great, spiritual experience and so much fun. We need more women building their own future.

THE THREE BIGGEST CHALLENGES I FACE

In my profession, the first challenge I face is helping people get over their fear of going to a lawyer in the first place. They understand that they need help but they just don't know how to find someone or how to reach out to someone.

The second challenge I face is the public's perception of how cases work through the judicial system. People have a false perception of how legal cases progress and the amount of time involved in resolving a legal matter. Television shows add to the incorrect information people have about the legal field. Sometimes people have a preconceived idea about how certain things work and if it doesn't work the way they see it happen on television, they are confused and get frustrated. We do our best to explain the process upfront so people have realistic expectations.

The third challenge is the Internet – it's actually my number one challenge as far as priority level. While it is a useful tool to gather information, there is too much false information that people find when searching for answers to legal questions. People come into my office after they read something on the Internet and they already have what they believe to be the answer to their legal question so essentially, they are looking for us to verify what they found on the Internet. We explain to them that the information they read online is incorrect, but the response we receive from them is, "It was on the Internet, so it must be true." We explain that much of the legal information found on the Internet is placed there by non-lawyers so it is not accurate. It really bothers me that so many people are so misinformed.

This has become a huge problem because the average person thinks that by gathering information online they are helping themselves and saving some money in the process. What they are really doing is hurting themselves. If they would talk to a lawyer at the onset of the problem, we would be able to set them in the right direction. A lawyer isn't just necessary when you are in the middle of a problem; a lawyer is beneficial in helping you avoid a potential problem.

For example, a lawyer can prevent problems during the purchase of a home, especially when buying a first home in North Carolina, if the lawyer is consulted from the very beginning. People should have an attorney review a real estate contract before they sign it because they're making the biggest investment of their lives at that time. Many times, as attorneys, people only come to us with questions after they have already signed some of their rights away. I have had the same disappointing conversations with many homebuyers after they had given up some of their legal rights by entering a contract before they found problems with the house.

For example, let's say that your house has a defect in the construction that causes water intrusion and mold-related issues. It would have been more beneficial to spend the money to have an expert tell you what is in your contract. Now, after signing your rights away without a lawyer, you may have limited recourse and still owe money on your house. The issue could have been avoided if you had consulted with a lawyer before signing that contract.

In my business, our consultation process is very streamlined. As lawyers, we always begin with a conflict check on the parties involved. In other words, you can't represent people on different sides of an issue. For instance, you can't represent a landlord in an action against the tenant if you already represented the tenant in an action, if it relates to the same subject matter. After we verify we have no conflicts, we complete an intake form and review the information. My office offers a reduced rate for the first 30 minutes of a consultation to make our legal services affordable for all.

One reason for our firm's success, is that if we can teach someone how to resolve a problem himself or herself, we'll tell them how to do it. If we don't think it's worth their while to hire us, we'll tell them that to. On the other hand, if they have a big, complicated case, we tell them that they need a lawyer and hope they'll select us. Our offer of a reduced rate for the first 30 minutes of a consultation is both helpful and challenging, because many law firms offer free consultations. Many times, when lawyers offer a free consultation, they are simply trying to get the client to retain them and they don't really give any concrete advice during the consultation. We give people concrete advice about their situation when they come in to talk to us for the first time.

I have taught many people how to go handle their own case in small claims court. I love nothing more than to hear afterwards about how well it went – they tell me how they won their case and tell me how happy they are about the advice that we gave to them. Many clients come back to us because they had a good experience or they'll give our name to somebody else. That is how we have grown our business over the years.

It's an interesting experience to be a lawyer. Sometimes, believe it or not, you can resolve a big problem for someone in a 30-minute consultation. You meet with them for half an hour and they walk out of your office feeling relieved and happy. They understand their options and they know how to handle the problem or they realize that it's not really a problem. That's one of the things that satisfies me about my business.

TURNING OBSTACLES INTO OPPORTUNITIES

If you have a creative side, you look at things differently, especially if someone says that you can't do something a certain way. Rules of Civil Procedure govern lawsuits in both federal and state court. Sometimes, these rules are not very clear and it creates situations in which one part of the lawsuit could be subject to more than one interpretation. Often you will first see it as an obstacle and think, "I can't make this motion" or "I can't take care of this sort of thing." If you just look at that obstacle in a creative way, quite often, you can turn it into a resolution that you didn't think was possible.

An obstacle is always an opportunity to achieve something and to make it work. Usually, I have found that when one door closes it's for a reason, and another door opens based on what you do next. Rather than crawling into a hole and saying, "Oh, I can't do this" or "These approaches won't work," many times, if you are just creative, you will find a way to make it work. That's the basis of the tagline on our website, 'Lawyers Who Think Outside the Box.'

Truly, that is the creative side of what we do. Instead of saying, "Okay, in every case you go through this process and do it this way," we try a new approach. Sometimes that can be tremensdously successful. You should not allow a bad situation or a negative lawyer on the other side of a case to intimidate you. I think, "Oh, this person never smiles and this person is never cordial" but by the time the case is over, it will be my goal to have a good relationship with this person. I view it as a challenge and as an opportunity to create change.

As I said before, when I graduated law school, I worked for a large law firm with almost 500 lawyers. It was the largest law firm in Indiana. I didn't know anybody there and I hadn't attended law school in Indiana so I had to take the Indiana Bar Exam. At the time, I was thinking, "My gosh, how am I ever going to do this? I don't know if I can pass the Bar Exam. I don't know if I can do this kind of work." I didn't let that get me down — I set my mind to what needed to be done and I did it. When I moved to North Carolina, I went to work for another large law firm. It wasn't as large as the one in Indiana but it was one of the biggest firms in the state. I stayed with this law firm for a long time and little by little, I received large cases to work on. By 2008, I started my own law firm.

After I finished law school, I never imagined it was possible that I would be successful at owning my own law firm. I wasn't always as positive as I am today. I had to retrain my brain and learn to be confident in what I'm doing. I finally worked up the courage to do it. The last seven and a half years have been the best experience of my life. I have a great group of people that work for me, and we work hard to make coming to work fun. We even have doggy Fridays, where one of us brings our dogs to work and provide us with animal therapy.

Once I finally believed that owning my own law firm was possible and I went after it, I made it work. If I had kept my old mindset, I wouldn't have dared to try. I would have said, in the back of my mind, "Boy, you know what? I wish I could have done that, or tried that. Maybe it would have worked." Instead, I took the attitude that, "I'm going to make it work. If it doesn't work, I tried. I gave it my best shot." I just remembered my dad saying, "Always do the best you can." Those are some of the greatest words of wisdom. I think that children want that type of affirmation from their parents, especially from their dad.

COMMON MYTHS

I think that women still have the mentality that this is more of a man's world and they can't be the main income earner. Somehow, some women feel inferior and think that they can't do certain things. Again, that goes back to your mental state and having the positivity in your head that you can actually go ahead and do whatever you want. I also think that if you are starting a business, you think, "Well, I have to have money to start the business. How am I going to get the money? There is just no way." Well, there is a way if you sit down and think about it. There are always options available. I believe if you truly want to make something happen, you can.

Since the economy has changed so much, many lawyers have moved into other practice areas — I'm a good example of that shift. When I first began practicing law, all I handled was environmental litigation. They were super fun cases and the litigation experience was great but I hadn't worked in many other practice areas. As a lawyer, people often think, "Oh, I can't learn a new thing," or, "Oh, that's going to be too difficult." As time went on, I just kept learning and found out that I love taking classes and researching new areas law. I wanted to teach myself how to invest in real estate and the stock market so I took classes and researched the subject then I purchased a home and rented it. I wanted to do it, so I did it.

We all have that ingrained idea that we can't do certain things when we actually can do them if we want to do them. The problem is that we have obstacles in our head that tell us, "It's too hard to do that." I thought that about law school. The obstacles in my head were saying, "I don't know if I can do that. Law school is for men and I don't know if I can get through it. I don't know how I will pay for it." I got scholarships and I borrowed money, but I did it. I paid back every cent of those loans and it felt great when I wrote that last loan payment check. It seemed like it was never going to end, like a mortgage payment, but sometimes that's what you have to do if you want to get to your goals.

BALANCING RELATIONSHIPS

As far as family and your significant others, the biggest challenge in owning a business is that it's a 24/7 thing. If you have an entrepreneurial spirit, it's really hard to put it down and let it go. With the advent of technology, it's very hard to keep away from your iPhone, iPad, and computer. You really have to find and take time to spend with the people who are important to you. That time is just as important as the time that you spend at work.

If you're courteous to people, whether it is your client or someone who waits on you at the grocery store, you make a difference in those people's lives just by treating them with respect. Anyone who comes to work in my law firm is told this before they're hired, but they also see it in the others who work for me. Within our office, everyone has to be a team. We have to build and weave an internal network. Everyone needs to pitch in to make it work. I always tell people that if I go into the bathroom and there's no toilet paper, I'm going to put on a new roll myself. I'm not going to come out and ask someone else, "Would you please put the toilet paper on the roller?" I think that when you act like that, people respect you. When everyone works as a group, it's more fun to come to work. The more fun it is to come to work, the more you will enjoy the day. The harder people work for you, the more successful the team will be. I don't want to talk badly about people that I have worked for in my career but I did learn many lessons in how not to treat people.

I always told myself that if I ever owned a business, I wouldn't do certain things. I'd refuse to treat people in certain ways because experiencing that myself had a negative effect on me. When you build relationships with people, whether it's people who work for you, friends or family members, it's important to treat them well. When you make them feel good about themselves, you're giving them a better quality of life. I love nothing more than when someone leaves our office after a meeting and he or she is glad they came in to see us.

I was talking earlier about one of the challenges that we face in getting people to realize that they need to consult a lawyer. When you consult a lawyer, it's because you have a problem, unless you are starting a business. You need something and that's intimidating. Therefore, when someone leaves our office and that person says, "Thank you so much for the help you gave us. I really enjoyed talking to you," it's really great. It's as if you turned them around. They were afraid to come see you in the first place but by the time they leave they feel relieved and comforttable. I think that's a critical part of the legal practice and, at the end of the day, it makes you feel good.

DAILY 'TO DO' LISTS

If you are a creative person, making lists is extremely important because you tend to have ideas floating around in your head all of the time — sometimes those are your best ideas. I'm more of a night owl so I like to stay up. I get some of my best ideas after I've gone to sleep. I'll wake up at around three or four in the morning with ideas about work. I don't know why but I've always been that way. Because of that, I always have my phone with me or I have a pad of paper so I can make notes of my ideas when I have them.

Every day, when I get to the office and even before leaving the office for the day, I write things down on my list. Keeping that list keeps me focused. Without the list, I wouldn't remember things. In my line of work, there are court deadlines, so my to-do-list is always in a dynamic state. In fact, sometimes I think, which is probably true for everyone, that all I do is re-write my list. Making the list helps you solidify in your head what you need to accomplish and what your priorities are for that day. I'm sure that if I didn't write my lists, I wouldn't be nearly as productive.

Sometimes I will make my list on my computer. That way, it can sync to my other electronic devices. As long as you have the list backed up on iCloud, even if you lose your iPhone or iPad, you don't need to worry. Technology makes it possible for me to have my list with me at all times with a reminder of what important tasks need to be done.

THE IMPORTANCE OF PASSION

You have to be passionate about what you do. Don't pretend that you like what you are doing as your chosen career. You need to be honest with yourself. If someone is going through the motions and he or she act as if they enjoy their job but they don't, it will always show.

I am a firm believer that passion comes from within your soul and I think if you really like doing what you do, it shows to the rest of the world. You won't even need to say, "I love what I do," because your actions show that you do. I worked for the big law firms and big businesses but there really wasn't a time when I thought that maybe I didn't like my career but it did feel as if something was missing. Once I started my own firm, I finally realized that the problem wasn't my drive and creativity; I had just been stymied and held back by those environments.

Not everything that I try works out, but some things do. Once I was able to say, "Hey, we are going to do it this way. We are going to try this," it felt great. I was finally able to be creative. I started to really enjoy what I was doing I started seeing people satisfied with how things turned out. Whether I talked to them for 30 minutes or handled their case for two years, they became part of me. I think the passion started showing. I think the bottom line is you need to love what you do and you need to have passion for it. You can't fake it because that shows. If you don't love what you are doing, then find out what you do love, and do it.

Not everyone finds out what he or she loves to do, so I feel fortunate that I was able to figure it out and go for it. There was a time I thought, "Maybe this isn't the right thing for me," but once I had my own business and started working creatively, it made a huge difference in my life.

It's easy to blame others for your unhappiness or your failures but it all begins and ends with you. Take responsibility for your successes and failures. It's time to stop trying to blame everybody else for the things you can't control because there are so many more things in your life that you can control. If you get lazy or hold yourself back, then that responsibility rests on you and nobody else. I don't do well with excuses. I get frustrated when people say, "I never did this before." My response is, "Well, I understand that but you can still figure it out. Do your best and give it a shot." That lack of confidence sometimes hurts people.

The beginning is the hardest time in any venture. I lived life thinking that I never want to look back and say, "I wish I would have." When I was getting ready to launch out on my own many people said, "Oh, it will take time but in a year or two you will be saying, "Why didn't I do it sooner?" They were right. It's true. If you don't believe in yourself, you are never going to try. It took time for me to build my confidence. It didn't happen overnight, but when it did happen, it was as if a wall had been torn down. All of a sudden I was thinking, "Man, I can actually do this!" It's very rewarding to know that you built something.

THE CLIENT EXPERIENCE SAYS IT ALL

I always tell people that the client experience starts from the person at the front desk. She does everything from answering the phone to receiving the payment in the back from my office manager. I have very strict rules. I don't want the phone to ring constantly; you need to answer it by a certain number of rings. You also have to treat everyone equally, whether it is just a thirty-minute consultation or a lengthy case that will cost a person thousands of dollars in legal fees. Everyone is treated the same way and that's been part of the success of my business. People really appreciate that. In the big law firms that I worked for, the attorneys often only accepted the cases that brought a lot of money into the firm. That is one reason why the entire economic climate has changed so much for the big firms.

Regardless of the case size, big or small, the attorney has to understand that everyone is entitled to be treated as a human being — they deserve honesty. Sometimes people don't have a case when they are in the wrong. If that's the situation, tell them that. Sometimes the information that you relay isn't what someone wants to hear but you need to be honest with people and tell them what you think. You don't find honesty everywhere and not all lawyers care about their clients – a lot of abuse happens in the world from workers in many different industries that take advantage of people in need.

That happens a lot in emergencies with the insurance industry and it is so irritating to see it happen. For instance, North Carolina has many landlord tenant issues because of the large number of apartments located here. Often, these apartments have water leaks that go unrepaired, and cause mold or other hazardous conditions. It's awful to see landlords take advantage of someone whose apartment has been damaged. We work hard to be sure that those tenants' rights are protected. I think that those abusers simply don't like what they are doing. I don't know how they could love their jobs. The people who are struggling have so much stress and, when someone takes advantage of them, it just makes their situation worse. Some people don't like lawyers, period. My response to that idea is always, "If everyone in the world did what was right, you wouldn't need a lawyer." Lawyers are needed because people don't do the right thing or they take advantage of others; someone needs to be an advocate for the victim.

Unfortunately, in this world, it's easier to complain than to compliment. In any profession, you will find the good and the bad. There is nothing worse for people than to discover they need someone to help them with an issue, and once they actually consult an attorney, they feel uncomfortable. It's hard to tell a perfect stranger what is happening in your personal life. You need someone who will make you feel at ease. That comes not only from the person you are asking to help you but also from the surroundings.

This is why I designed our office in a very relaxing way. When people come in the door, they see attractive artwork in a calm surrounding. There's nothing better than hearing from someone, "I'm so glad that I came in here. I feel so good about how I was treated." That makes me feel good at the end of the day. I love that feeling. It confirms what I have known for a long time, I truly enjoy being a lawyer and helping people. This is what I was born to do.

(This content should be used for informational purposes only. It does not create an attorney-client relationship with any reader and should not be construed as legal advice. If you need legal advice, please contact an attorney in your community who can assess the specifics of your situation.)

8

GRIDIRON GUIDANCE

by Matthew Trapani, Esq.

Matthew Trapani, Esq.
Trapani Law Firm
Allentown, Pennsylvania
www.ltlaw.com

Attorney Matthew Trapani devotes his legal career to representing the seriously injured and their families across the state of Pennsylvania. Located in Allentown, PA, Trapani handles a variety of catastrophic personal injury cases including automobile and tractor-trailer accidents, premises liability, medical malpractice, liquor liability violations and wrongful death litigation.

Born in Easton, PA, Matthew graduated from Easton Area High School as a varsity football letterman. He continued his schooling at the Pennsylvania State University, where he earned both his undergraduate and law degrees. Throughout his time in law school, Trapani served as a member of the Corpus Juris Society. After graduating from the Penn State Dickinson School of Law, Matthew could not wait to begin his career representing those who had been wrongfully injured, in order to support his local community.

Matthew Trapani is one of the youngest lawyers to become a certified life member of the Multi-Million Dollar Advocates Forum. The forum is a group of attorneys, made up of less than 1% of all lawyers in the United States, who have recorded verdicts, awards and settlements of $2 Million or more.

GRIDIRON GUIDANCE

GROWING UP GRIDIRON

I grew up in Easton, Pennsylvania, which is in the area we call the Lehigh Valley; Easton, Allentown, and Bethlehem are the three prominent cities. I currently live in Bethlehem. My office is in Allentown, and my parents still live in Easton. This is where I've spent the majority of my life. My network reaches back to my high school teachers, football coaches, family, and friends, all of whom live around here. This has given me a built-in client base and a trustworthy reputation from day one.

I went to the Pennsylvania State University for both my undergraduate work and law school at the Penn State Dickenson School of Law. I grew up a fan of the football team there as well, so I couldn't leave the place once I was there – I spent seven years at

Penn State. Without knowing it, I was doing a lot of networking at that time. I made a lot of life-long friends at Penn State who have gone on to have successful careers. I'm starting to realize that when your network starts doing big things, it helps you along the way.

At the time I started applying to different law schools, I realized that I could get Penn State football tickets for three more years – I knew that it was the place for me. They also had a pretty good reputation in the legal community, especially here in Pennsylvania, so it was kind of a no-brainer. I'm a big family guy; so staying close to home has always felt like the right move for me.

It might seem a little cliché, but boy oh boy, you carry the life lessons learned on the football field forever. I played some other sports, not as intensely, and I always go back to the lessons of football. It's the ultimate team sport. Ten guys are blocking just so one is able to pick up some yards or score a touchdown. Football taught me: self-discipline, commitment, respect, dedication, teamwork and toughness. When my clients come in, I look at them as if they are now part of my team. I treat them the same way that I treated my teammates - with a lot of respect. You'd do anything for your teammates, and you will work your hardest to be there for them. That's my thought process.

MY PERSONAL PLAYBOOK

I'm single. I haven't married yet, and that is a calculated decision. I'm big on career and wealth building, and taking risks earlier in life seemed like the prudent move. In my mind, you have youth as a parachute. As soon as you have kids and a mortgage, you can't take nearly as many financial risks.

I do a lot of investing, especially in real estate. Protecting my future wealth is one of the hobbies that I'm most passionate about. It probably sounds a little nerdy, but nothing gets me quite as excited as sitting down and reading over a real estate investment or an angel investment in a startup business. I like to invest in multi-family residential units, as well as commercial real estate. I invest in the stock market, and I also participate in angel investing and backing start-up businesses with 'seed round' investing. I do want to raise a family someday. I am a family guy, and I've always had those plans as something I'll do in my later thirties, once all of my investments start paying off. Truly, one of my favorite hobbies is turning small piles of money into larger piles of money; but spending time with my parents, sister, brother-in-law and three nieces is always the most important priority of mine.

I've entered the world of investing fairly recently, only because it takes a long time to finish law school and make a little bit of money as an associate, so that I could go out and start my own law firm. Now that my law firm is finally profitable, I can become an investor with my law firm proceeds. After working through that process, I'm hoping that those investments will turn into their own sources of income. Rather than just working for money to spend as a consumer, I'd like to have some financial freedom through other sources of income, and let my money work for me. Financial education and knowledge is key and I continue to learn on a daily basis even though I'm through with my formal education.

WHY LAW?

I'm far from a perfect guy. Let me just say that my youthful rebellion phase was a bit more intense than most, and there were times when I needed a lawyer to help me out of little troubles as a teenager. You know, typical teenager nonsense, though I didn't really get into major problems. I didn't always feel like I was my lawyer's priority, so later on, I decided that I would never let any of my clients feel like they weren't a priority. I've never let them feel that way, not once. To this day, I still try to run my personal injury practice that way.

A lot of bad things can happen to people, and my firm gets some big cases, in terms of really severe injuries. We also get relatively minor injuries, such as whiplash or back pain. I work hard to make sure that every one of my clients feels like they're my most important client. This particular value is due to some of those experiences that I went through when I was younger. Those early lessons in prioritizing are always in the back of my mind.

CULTIVATING COURAGE

That sort of thing is perfect for turning lemons into lemonade. I mean, you live those experiences that shape you and your future. You embrace events that might have been seen as negative at the time, so that you can take away positives from those experiences. So, I try to be optimistic and learn from both my mistakes and the mistakes of others.

Overall, you've got to have courage if you want to be able to do the big things in life. At age 29, I started my own law firm; many people probably thought it was a little too early. I had done a couple trials, worked through some appeals, and I had a few years of legal experience, so I took that jump earlier than most people would have. By age 32, I won my first Multi-Million dollar personal injury award. At the end of the day, if you're not willing to take some risks, you won't end up where you want to be. Courage is key.

ADVICE TO FUTURE LEADERS IN THE LAW

Besides courage, it's really important to have mentors, especially in your first few years. I still remember walking into the courtroom on that first day; nobody learns everything they need to know in law school or while taking the bar exam. I wasn't even sure whether to stand on the right side or the left – no one had told me up until that point. Hopefully, your mentors will be willing to coach you, so you can glean some of the experience they've gained over the years. Your boss should have a track record of success, someone who's also willing to teach you along the way. I certainly got lucky – I wouldn't have been able to do half of what I've accomplished without great mentors.

I also highly recommend reading biographies about other lawyers and businessmen and women. Reading through their experiences and hardships will help you gain the courage you need to take big steps forward. Additionally, while everyone must learn from mistakes, they don't have to be your mistakes. The best part about reading biographies of successful people is that you can learn from other's mistakes without having to make them yourself. I always try and read a couple of books when I get some free time. It's good education, and also good relaxation.

Again, going back to courage, I think people are too patient nowadays with their five-year and ten-year goals. When it comes to wanting to get out on your own and start your own business, law firm or corporation, start working on it tonight. Why wait till tomorrow? Start figuring out your marketing plan, your location, your client base, your back-up plan (plan B). Put pen to paper. Don't just sit around and say, "It will all work out for me in my five-year plan and my ten-year plan." I think you need to hit the ground running – don't wait another day if you have big plans. Start working on them now.

FULFILLING YOUR DREAMS

In this line of work, it's easy to allow yourself to become overworked, or not make enough time for some of the other things in life that are important. You've got to focus on your health - take a little time to stay in shape and eat right. My old mentors at one law firm did not do that, and they had some serious health problems later on. I promised myself that would never happen to me. My practice is important, and my clients are important, but I have to make my health just as important.

You must also make time for friends and family. If you're not doing that, you have to ask yourself, "Why am I doing all of this hard work anyway?" So, every day I try to get to the gym, eat right, and spend a little time with friends or family. Also, you need a couple of hobbies that you love for yourself. You have to be a little bit selfish with your time.

Besides my law practice and investing, my alma mater is important too. I went to Penn State, and met many of my great friends there. So we still get together, do the tailgate thing, and go to a couple of games every year. The team is not always great, but it's always like a little family reunion for us, and that's something I really look forward to. You need to make time for all of those other things that are important, in addition to your business. That's what I look for when I'm looking for fulfillment in life.

It's also important to have a little fun and adventure. I'm not afraid to travel into different counties in Pennsylvania: Philadelphia, Pittsburgh, Scranton, Harrisburg, State College, etc. As a young single guy, sometimes getting out of the area and going on a road trip for a case is a lot of fun.

SURROUND YOURSELF WITH SUCCESSFUL PEOPLE

At my orientation at Penn State, even though I couldn't tell you the name of the speaker (he was probably a dean or something), he told us that the number one skill we were going to learn was networking. He said that those who take advantage of it would have success long into their future. I'm not going to say that, as an 18-year-old kid, I really believed everything he had to say, but looking back on that statement, it's so true.

I firmly believe that networking is the most important skill that you will ever have. You need to have great social skills when you meet people who are going to do big things, and who are like-minded. I keep a Microsoft Word list of people that I meet, if I think they're intelligent or go-getters. Sometimes these are guys with deep pockets, who might want to invest in a project later on. I stay in touch with these people. I take trips to visit them, and I send them little gifts, because a well-developed network is a tremendous asset. I don't think people truly realize the opportunities that might just pass them by, or if they even realize what they have right in front of them. The power of networking is phenomenal, and even though I'm young, I have already seen its tremendously positive effects on my own life.

I constantly tell people about the importance of this skill. In my twenties, I was networking and I didn't even know it. I had a pretty busy social life. I never passed up an opportunity on the weekend to go out and do something social. I always had a shore house in my twenties and a lot of friends who lived in Manhattan and Philly would come visit for entertainment and social purposes. What's funny is that these same people are now business partners, investors, or clients of mine. Or I'm a client of theirs, and we have some great stories about our crazy Friday and Saturday nights back in our twenties.

The network that I created while doing those things is pretty incredible, especially because I wasn't yet aware of the long-term benefit that networking would bring. My parents might have been yelling at me, telling me I shouldn't be spending every weekend out hootin'- and - hollerin' around the shore with my buddies, or going to every Penn State football game. In hindsight, though, I was creating one heck of a network that I'm very proud of, and that has really given me a lot of positive benefits in the long run. I know it's only going to benefit me more throughout my life.

Now that I've realized networking is such an important tool to have in my tool belt, it's something that I work hard at, and I actually find myself networking for other people. I try to bring parties together. I say, "You know what, I know this friend, and he could really help out your business. Let me send an introductory email." So, I do more networking for other people because I know, at the end of the day, it can only be positive karma for me.

It's so interesting how all of this came into play. I learned the power of networking, really, from a friend of mine who also went to Penn State, and then he went on to Vanderbilt Law School. He's now an attorney in Manhattan. When you look at his network, it's pretty tremendous. He has demonstrated to me how networking can be beneficial to him, both from a financial and a social standpoint. He also taught me that bringing other people together can be a huge benefit for everyone involved.

I've just recently introduced a new friend to the owner of a business in which I'm invested. It's fun and exciting to see the circle come together, and the good connections come to fruition. It's a win-win for everybody, and it's just using the power we have at our fingertips. It's amazing how many people don't understand, and don't use, the resources they already have.

BE READY TO PAY THE PRICE

Many people in my industry can have big egos. They sometimes think they know it all. I try to have the exact opposite opinion - to never let my ego get in the way of decisions. I'm willing to listen and learn from anyone, although I will judge that advice by way of the credentials and previous success gained by that person. Additionally, I've found that the best place to gain advice and knowledge is in the biographies and autobiographies of great leaders, businessmen and women and lawyers.

Let me tell you a quick funny story. Sam Walton, the former owner of Wal-Mart, wrote a book, called Made in America, that's not as popular as it should be, especially considering that this businessman basically built the biggest store in America or in the world. He once received a letter from some gentlemen who were creating a similar store down in South America. Basically, they just wanted to talk shop, talk business, and network a little bit, so they sent a letter to every CEO and board member of all the big stores at that time: Macy's, Niemen Marcus, K-Mart, and Wal-Mart. They only received one reply - from Sam Walton - who was the owner and CEO of the biggest store in America at that point in time. Sam, the only responder, invited them to his home for a great meeting and a great dinner. Halfway through the dinner, the men from South America started thinking, "Hey, we didn't even get to ask Sam any questions yet, because he's been asking us so many questions about our business, our practices, and our procedures!"

They maintained the relationship, and at some point later on, they invited Sam down to South America to visit them. He went down with his family for a family vacation. The gentlemen in South America received a phone call from the police saying, "We have this American in custody; he says he's with you. We found him crawling around in a store on his hands and his knees with a measuring tape, and we arrested him."

They thought Sam was crazy. They bailed him out of jail and said, "Sam, what are you doing?" He told them, "You know, your aisles are closer together than mine, and they're a couple of inches lifted off the ground at my stores, and I wanted to see if you guys knew something that I didn't." So, one of the richest, most powerful men in the world, was crawling around on his hands and knees on the floor with a measuring tape, to see if these up-and-coming guys in South America knew something that he didn't!

Always be prepared to pay the price to get ahead. Be willing to get your hands dirty, get on your hands and knees, put your ego in check, and outwork anybody in whatever field you may be in. I always carry that little story with me.

From time to time, I find myself in a situation where I should be taking the time to research something relating to the business, but I want to spend some time relaxing or watching a Penn State football game. That's when I think of Sam, and I say to myself, "No, I've got to be willing to do little things." Ultimately, that will separate me from the other lawyers and other businessmen. I put my ego in check, roll up my sleeves, and get to work.

My hard work has already paid off. At age 32, I'm one of the youngest lawyers that is a certified life member of the Multi-Million Dollar Advocates Forum. The forum is a group of lawyers, made up of less than 1% of all attorneys in the United States, who have recorded settlements, awards, and verdicts of $2 Million or more. I'm very proud to have reached such a milestone so early in my career and I look forward to building on this accomplishment in the future.

GIVE MORE TO MAKE MORE

I'm also a big believer in giving to charity, and giving back to the community. The more I give to charity, and the more I help the youth in my community, the more that success seems to come my way. That relates back to my other sports saying, which is, "The harder I work, the luckier I get." In my mind, truer words have never been spoken.

When I write down the reasons why I want to be successful, being able to give back to the community and to help others who may not have had the same opportunities that I've been given, turns out to be the number one reason. Being able to continually give back is really important to me. It's something that I always want to be able to do.

I like to help out with the community youth football league, although currently, I don't coach because I don't have the time for it. I am close with the coaching staff, and I like to be something of a mentor to some of those kids. Also, when I get the opportunity, I do some pro-bono legal representation for the youth athletic community.

In the future, I actually see myself coaching. If I did have a couple boys, years from now, I would make sure that they learned the correct techniques in their youth. I look forward to being an elementary football coach, putting some young men on the right path while teaching them the important life lessons that come along with football. That's on my to-do list.

Leaving behind a legacy is important. It could be summed up by this saying: "You actually die twice." You die once when you pass away and then once again at the last time your name is ever spoken. Someday, I hope that my legacy will be looked upon in a positive light - that I have helped a lot of people. I like helping the younger generation for those reasons, to get some people on the right track. At times I'm dealing with youth either because of an accident or some real trouble, and I try to not only be a lawyer at that moment; I also try to be a bit of a mentor and give the best advice that I can. Sometimes parents have told me, "You are sending the right message – you setting them straight means more than hearing it from me." I always relish that opportunity.

CONFLICTS OF THE HEART

We all need mentors. I met my first legal mentor when I was in law school. He is an attorney, and a family friend in New Jersey. New Jersey is one of the states where the Catholic priest scandal was pretty prevalent. He's Catholic, and so am I. As it turned out, his old priest was involved, and even some of his friends had been molested, or had been abused by a priest. Even though he was an altar boy, he never knew anything about it. So all these years later, while in his fifties, he started finding out about these hushed-up scandals. These stories came up when I was doing my first internship in law school with him.

His practice swarmed with new clients. The work snowballed, because all of these parish members from his community knew him and eventually became his clients. That was 11 years ago. I still see him at church on most Sundays, and we'll end up chatting about our practices. It's great to get advice from him on my cases; he's still doing nothing but Catholic abuse cases, which are a lot more prevalent in New Jersey than they are in Pennsylvania, due to the state laws.

I don't have a lot of those cases now, but I was very involved in the beginning. That was the majority of my caseload for a few summers in law school. It was incredible as a first legal experience, spread across the news stations with HBO specials on that topic.

It was very interesting to be a part of something like that, for a number of reasons. One, I got to be involved in cases regarding moral transgressions early on in my career. Two, I was (and am) a devout Catholic, but as one of a number of attorneys, I was helping to sue the Catholic Church on behalf of our clients. Attorneys always owe zealous representation to our clients, and I had to represent them to the best of my ability, even though there's that moral factor, and even though I am also true to the Catholic Church and believe in it. I learned a lot through that situation.

A few years later, suddenly the Jerry Sandusky scandal appeared. As I mentioned earlier, I'm very involved with Penn State athletics, since it's both my undergraduate and my law school alma mater. Once again, I was right in the middle of this current event. ESPN radio did an interview. Maybe they had seen on my website that I had legal experience with the Catholic abuse scandal, and also that I'm a big Penn State supporter, so they wanted to interview me regarding my thoughts on the Sandusky scandal. I'm very careful to not call it the 'Penn State scandal.' I really believe that Jerry

Sandusky was a pretty terrible guy, and I hope that the plaintiffs, who were so severely abused by him, were justly compensated.

It's sad. It's incredibly horrible. Yes, sometimes in this profession, an attorney will be put between a rock and a hard place. At that point, your true colors will show. I truly believe that we need personal injury and wrongful death attorneys to make society a safer place. This is one of the major roles that I play in society. I'm going to tell you a few stories about that.

MAKING SOCIETY SAFER THROUGH LITIGATION

The Catholic abuse scandal and the Jerry Sandusky scandal are very high-profile cases, and created really provocative headlines, but lots of important cases don't make that kind of splash. Making society safer is something that's important to me. It's one of the cogs in the wheel of my law firm (The Trapani Law Firm) that I take very seriously; it's something that I think my firm does a great job with. I'm proud of some of the changes we've already made in policies and procedures cases that featured big corporations as the defendants. Hopefully, I can make this world a little bit of a safer place while I'm at work in it.

I represent clients who have had serious injuries: brain damage, scarring from burns, spinal cord injuries, birth injuries, broken bones, and (unfortunately) even death. That's just to name a few. These injuries are typically life changing, and the result of another person's negligence or reckless actions. The most frequent types of lawsuits in my practice involve automobile and truck accidents, medical malpractice, product liability, premises liability, and construction accidents.

Although I can't undo any physical harm for my clients, it's my job to get them and their families back on their feet - to make them as whole as possible. That is truly important to me. As I told you, I look at my clients as a part of my team, and I'm going to do everything possible on their behalf. I take this responsibility very seriously, and put everything I have into my client's representation.

Unfortunately, many cases involve the wrongful death of another person. No amount of money can bring back the loved one lost in a tragedy; however, the resulting compensation usually helps children pay for future educational expenses, and provides support to a widow who is faced with the difficult task of raising a family by herself. Personal injury lawsuits are necessary in order to hold individuals and companies accountable for reckless and negligent conduct. I hope I'm making society a safer place. I typically recover lost wages, medical expenses, fair compensation for pain and suffering, as well as future medical expenses that a client may endure.

I've been dealing with insurance companies since my time back in law school, and throughout my career, including the Catholic scandal and the Jerry Sandusky scandal. I believe that insurance companies are focused on profits rather than on fair dealings with their clients. They report billions of dollars of profits on a yearly basis, and their main goal is to minimize the amount paid to each injured party. That is the reason why, if you've been injured, you need an advocate - an experienced personal injury or wrongful death attorney, who is able to handle a suit against the billion-dollar insurance corporation.

For instance, as soon as I am contacted and retained by a client, I will send out representation notices to any and all insurance carriers who may be involved. I tell them that all conversations and communications need to be funneled through me and not through my client. The reason for that is because most insurance companies try to get statements before a lawyer is involved with a client, and people sometimes say the wrong thing. Once I'm involved, I won't let my clients say the wrong thing.

The person who calls in the accident, or the person who I represent, may not have caused the accident. However, out of pure human instinct, they may feel compelled to run over and ask the injured party, "I'm so sorry, are you okay?" If that statement gets recorded or reiterated to an insurance company representative, the statement may be used to prove that you were negligent rather than just a good human being who was worried about another human being at that moment. A lot of times, the insurance representative tries to act like your best friend, they are trained to make people feel comfortable enough to say something that can hurt your case. That's why it's a good idea to immediately contact a personal injury attorney and have them handle all communications up to the point of a trial.

The truth is that the majority of personal injury and wrongful death cases settle prior to a jury trial. Thankfully, we do have a jury system in place that allows us to litigate claims in front of a jury of one's peers, if that is the route that needs to be taken. Litigation, throughout a jury trial, is a lengthy and expensive process. I've always believed that anyone who ends up in a jury trial must hire the most experienced medical and liability experts, but this gets expensive. Luckily for the client, my firm, along with most other personal injury firms, works on a contingency basis. Attorneys accept all of the risk of taking the case to trial, so we pay for all of the expenses up front. If we lose the trial, which rarely happens for me, the client would have no obligation to pay those out-of-pocket expenses that are incurred throughout the trial.

This allows everyone the ability to take a case to trial, regardless of his or her income level. No matter where they come from, or whom they know, the personal injury law firm will usually be able to take it to trial if the case so merits. In the end, personal injury attorneys are only paid if and when we win the case; then we take a percentage of the amount won according to our agreement. I think that this structure levels the playing field; it lets the personal injury lawyers, who are a lot smaller than the insurance companies, take all of the risk, roll the dice, and go to court in kind of a David vs. Goliath set-up. It enables everyday people, who couldn't otherwise challenge these massive insurance corporations, to at least have the chance to recover some part of what they've lost.

I represented a family for the loss of a loved one at a trailer home facility. A propane explosion killed my client after some excruciating pain and suffering. Sadly, as it turned out, the trailer home facility (which was owned by a large corporation) had documented proof of previous propane leaks. Even though a written report recommended that all of the propane lines should be dug up and replaced, because they were old and out of date, the company instead chose to only replace a couple of lines that had previously leaked. At the end of the day, their profitability was their number one concern. Many companies put profitability ahead of safety; so it's up to an attorney, like me, to make them think twice before making those types of decisions.

BEWARE OF SOCIAL MEDIA

Despite social media becoming so popular, my immediate advice is to stay away from social media concerning any legal issue. Insurance companies are known to search through social media records, looking through anything that would harm a person's case or their character in front of a jury. I have actually used social media to help gain a successful outcome in a Dram Shop case here in Pennsylvania. Dram Shop Law states that a bar or a restaurant may not serve a "visibly intoxicated person" in Pennsylvania. Whether or not a person is considered visibly intoxicated is the standard, and so many times the case is very fact-intensive; it depends on whether or not the person was slurring their speech or staggering. Maybe a video shows that the person tripped or fell over a chair, or a witness says that the person was extremely drunk "when he talked to me."

One of my clients was badly injured in a car accident as a result of a driver who was over-served at a very popular bar/restaurant franchise. The driver was served while visibly intoxicated. Using social media, I was able to obtain photographs of the bartender taking shots of liquor behind the bar, while on duty; basically, that's the person who is in charge of deciding whether or not the patron is visibly intoxicated or should be served another drink. Once I brought that social media evidence to light, the case settled very quickly. Due to that evidence, the bar didn't want to litigate, and the insurance company representatives did a complete turnaround; they wanted to settle that case as quickly as possible. It's my hope that this case will help make society a safer place. Specifically, it should make bar owners institute stricter policies and procedures with their employees pertaining to hiring practices, training, as well as the serving of alcohol.

At our initial consultation, I tell each client that they should refrain from posting photographs or status updates on any form of social media, updates that may in any way hurt their case or their character. Basically, I tell them if they can stay off social media completely, that's great. "Imagine that everything you're putting on social media is now being read to a jury or a judge who's deciding the outcome of your case before you post it." Hopefully that little test will either help them to not post, or to post something a lot smarter than they would have in the first place.

Let's say that other people (not my client) have posted videos or images that they captured at the site of the injury. Since news media sources often post scads of photographs after a big accident, the first thing that I do (after my client signs a fee agreement) is to start my investigation via Google, newspaper websites, and social media sites. It's faster than going to view the scene of an accident, which has probably already been cleaned up. I save those photographs to a database; even if they hurt my client's case, it's important to get your hands on everything that is available. The number one rule is to start collecting, investigating, and saving everything onto a database so that it's available when the time is right.

Whether or not those pieces of information or photographs can be used in the court of law or in a settlement negotiation, that's pretty fact-specific. You need to hear a lot more facts along the way, for each and every case, before you get a "yes" or "no" answer to the question of usefulness. Also, you need to know what you're trying to prove with that piece of evidence. More often than not, photographs will be allowed in through a rule of evidence, and many times they will help my case. There's also a motion that I could file with the court before trial, to keep out pieces of evidence, if I think they might be negative or hurt my case. This is called a 'Motion in Limine.'

On the flip side, for the client, it's important to have an attorney who is tech-savvy and Internet-savvy; someone who understands social media and grasps all of the tools that are available for investigation on the Internet. Experience is truly important, but not if you hire an attorney who's past his prime. If you're not yet in the litigation phase, your attorney doesn't have to turn anything over to anyone on the other side. If the opposing side doesn't know what's available in terms of evidence, then the goal may be to get to a settlement before that piece of evidence comes to light, which it absolutely will, once you get into litigation. So, when you hire a personal injury attorney or law firm, it's important to find an attorney who is savvy enough to find all available pieces of evidence on the Internet and elsewhere.

LEGAL DETAILS: LIMITED TORT VS. FULL TORT

While nobody can undo a tragedy, our legal system does allow an injured party to receive just financial compensation. In Pennsylvania, as well as some other states, there are two auto-mobile insurance options for tort actions: limited tort or full tort.

Limited tort is the cheaper option. People often come into my office after they've been injured in a car crash that wasn't their fault, and say, "I thought I had full coverage." In Pennsylvania, limited tort insurance bars people from pursuing compensation for pain and suffering. Many Pennsylvania drivers don't realize that it's possible to have exceptional coverage for property damage, medical expenses, even injuries caused to another, but the limited tort policy prohibits you from recovering money for your own injuries when you need it the most.

Their next statement is "But it wasn't my fault." Except for a few specific situations, fault doesn't matter if you have limited tort insurance. Even if you did nothing wrong and the crash was entirely someone else's fault, limited tort can prevent you from recovering compensation for your pain and suffering. People tend to choose the limited tort option because it's a little cheaper, sometimes $10 per month. For someone in the lower or middle class, saving $10 or $20 per month seems like the right choice because, you think, "This will never happen to me." This option can end up costing someone hundreds of thousands of dollars for an accident that they didn't even cause and wasn't their fault.

Many states don't have this option, and I wish that Pennsylvania did not. I'm always willing to schedule a free review for any clients or future clients to review their insurance policy. Their peace of mind doesn't cost them a red cent, except a few minutes of their time. Also, I highly recommend to all drivers in Pennsylvania (and any other state carrying this option) that they choose the full tort option rather than the limited tort option for their insurance policy.

IF YOU ARE INJURED

Number One: The first thing to do, if you've been in an accident, is to *get medical treatment*. You need to get evaluated at the emergency room immediately after the accident. Next, get follow-up treatment. Do all of the recommended physical therapies, occupational therapies, surgeries, pain management meetings, x-rays and CAT scans, or anything else that is required. You've got to do all of those treatments and tests precisely as the doctor says to do them, and at the medical facilities that he recommends. I'm not a doctor, so I don't give medical advice. However, as an attorney, I just want my clients to talk to the best doctors that we can locate, and do exactly what they tell you to do. My clients should be willing to work tremendously hard on their recovery, to get themselves back on their feet.

Number Two: Contact a personal injury or a wrongful death attorney as quickly as you can. If you don't know one, ask your friends, family, and co-workers. I'm a big believer in word-of-mouth referrals. Once an attorney is brought into the mix, we go into an investigation mode, and begin to gather all of the facts that we can get our hands on. Facts and evidence can disappear later on, or may not be available. Sometimes, just natural elements (rain, snow, and sleet) can get rid of some facts or evidence that we may be looking for. It's also possible that somebody on the other side of the case could be trying to cover something up, if they're responsible; more likely, there could be an attempt to cover up if a corporation is responsible. I have a team of experts, including private investigators and accident reconstructionists that I want to get working on the case as early as possible.

Number Three: Every one of my clients needs to do some homework. For instance, you will need to keep a journal of every place where you have received medical treatment, every drug taken, every event in your life that's been missed, every opportunity that won't come back, every bit of lost wages, and every job passed by during recovery. If you write down every detail in a journal, it will be helpful in your case, because your memory is never as sharp as you think it will be. Also, I need to receive regular updates - regular phone calls on your progress throughout your treatment. That may take a year or two, but I want to know every treatment that took place, how recovery is progressing, and all of the details – inside and out.

Number Four: At some point, I will put together a demand package that encompasses everything that my client has lost along their journey, like out-of-pocket medical expenses, pain and suffering, lost wages, and future medical expenses. As a team, we figure out those details together. Whether we choose to settle or negotiate a case, or litigate it through a jury trial, is a decision I always leave up to my client. I give advice to clients, but I don't make the decisions. At the end of the day, my client makes the decisions.

I feel very fortunate to get to know my clients and their families, and to develop a trusting relationship with them in order to understand how these accidents have turned their lives upside down; that's my job. I take it very seriously.

I've developed life-long relationships with lots of former clients, and nothing warms my heart more than the collection of heartfelt thank-you letters and Christmas cards that I've amassed over the years. I'm honored that they've allowed me to be apart of their team.

(This content should be used for informational purposes only. It does not create an attorney-client relationship with any reader and should not be construed as legal advice. If you need legal advice, please contact an attorney in your community who can assess the specifics of your situation.)

9

Living The American Dream

by Andrew J. Borsen, Esq.

Andrew J. Borsen, Esq.
Gambourg & Borsen, LLC
Fort Lee, New Jersey and NYC
www.rvgab.com

Andrew J. Borsen was born in St. Petersburg, Russia and emigrated to the United States in the mid 1990's. Borsen attended New England Law in Boston and graduated in 2003. Borsen's wife Morgan, is a doctor of physical therapy and has her own practice, MORE Physio, which caters to outpatient orthopedic injuries. They both live in New York.

Along with his partner, Roman, they are the firm Gambourg & Borsen LLC, a boutique law firm specializing in corporate transactions, commercial litigation, real estate, entertainment and international law. Half of Borsen's work is commercial litigation while the other half constitutes corporate transactions.

Borsen is an adjunct professor at Metropolitan College of New York, teaching in the Graduate School of Business. He began lecturing classes, such as Business Law and Employment Law and also instructs MCNY's Constructive Action program. The Constructive Action combines classroom instruction with practical, real world knowledge.

In addition to his legal practice, Borsen also invests in Broadway and Music Production. He was involved with On Golden Pond, Natasha and Pierre and the Great Comet of 1812 and Cosmic Opera. Additionally, he is part owner of a restaurant called Kitty's Canteen, on the Lower East Side.

LIVING THE AMERICAN DREAM

INTERNATIONAL ROOTS

Since arriving to the United State from St. Petersburg, Russia, my life has been a tremendous learning experience. As I slowly and methodically became more American in my outlook and perception, I was always mindful of my roots. Being both Russian and Jewish will always be a source of great pride.

In St. Petersburg, my family was involved in arts and politics. My aunt, Galina Staravoitova, was a notable politician who was unfortunately assassinated when I was younger. One of my grandfathers, Boris Ratser, was a notable poet while the other,

Alexander Lepyanskiy, was a famous singer. His fame resulted from translating and performing international songs from their original language into Russian. Back then, the Soviet Union did not allow foreign songs; and he was one of the first to gain notoriety from his performances. It was a very interesting but unstable time for my family in Russia.

Due to the prejudice against Jewish persons, which permeated and continues to permeate in Russian culture and society, my family had to move. While emigrating, we were forced to spend eighteen months in Italy as we patiently awaited permission to move to the U.S. I can't say that I had many complaints . . . pizza was quite a scarcity in Russia during the 80's.

When we finally made it to the U.S., and like many generations of immigrants who preceded us, I saw it as a wonderful opportunity. My first educational experience in the U.S. was in third grade in Bensonhurst, New York. It was a disastrous one. I was the only Russian in the school and was immediately identified as the object of jokes and derision. I had no friends and had low grades - my life was miserable.

As I began to think of ways to change my plight, the idea of conformity became apparent and appealing. After some diligent inquiries, I discovered New York Military Academy. A school where one wore uniforms, adhered to a stringent code of conduct, where all students started on similar footing and where no one was judged based on worldly possessions, appeared to be a solution. My parents enrolled me in N.Y.M.A. in 1993, when I was twelve years old.

My tenure at N.Y.M.A., which was supposed to last for one year turned into six. It turned out that I excelled in a disciplined environment. Everyone was on equal ground at military school; as long as you followed the rules you got ahead; I was good at following orders, graduating as a Head Cadet, Class Captain and Valedictorian of my class.

In 1999, immediately after graduation, I enrolled in Boston University in Boston, Massachusetts. In my family, there is a saying that the son becomes a doctor, and if he's a little slow, he becomes a lawyer. My parents really wanted me to be a doctor, however, after 10 days of being in the pre-med program, I switched to pre-law and have never looked back. I attended New England Law in Boston and graduated in 2003.

THE MAKING OF A LAWYER

Attending military school shaped me into who I am today. After shifting from my comfort zone of being part of a "high heeled" family in Russia, to leaving behind almost all material possessions and completely starting over in the U.S., N.Y.M.A. was the first place where I came into my own. Every cadet endured grueling physical, mental and emotional tasks while boarding a campus far away from their home. It was extremely challenging at most times, but these challenges created life long bonds among my peers. More credence was given to one's integrity instead of typical high school trivialities. This allowed me to excel both socially and academically.

Meeting my wife was another influential event in my life. When we met, I was working at a large New York defense firm, and she was working as a physical therapist at N.Y. Sports Med. After we were engaged I had an opportunity to either continue working for someone else or start my own practice. I certainly wanted to "go on my own" but had limited funds. I knew that I wouldn't be able to support myself at first while living in New York, but Morgan gave me the confidence and support to venture onward. I never wanted to jump without a nest, and she, along with my family and friends, helped weave my nest.

PRACTICING LAW: QUANTITY VS. QUALITY

After graduating from law school, I was hired by a prominent personal injury (PI) firm. PI firms, at times, are more concerned with "volume work," which values quantity of cases over quality of work. Each attorney was responsible for about 50 to 100 cases, which is considered a heavy caseload. During my first week I was assigned a deposition and a trial. I had never conducted a deposition, let alone a trial by myself. During my tenure at the PI firm, I took hundreds of depositions and handled numerous trials. I was exposed to work which most first and second year attorneys never get to experience and gained a good deal of confidence inside and outside the courtroom.

My next position was with a prominent New York defense firm. Most of my time with them consisted of sitting at a desk drafting contracts, motions, briefs and appeals. While it was not as exciting as the PI firm, it yielded a completely different work product. Each document had to be meticulously drafted with numerous rounds of revisions, edits and comments. It escalated the quality of my work and provided invaluable writing skills.

Between the two firms, a plaintiff's firm which honed my courtroom skills and a defense firm where I developed critical writing techniques, I received the benefit of a well rounded and practical education. Such education gave me the confidence to open up my own practice.

Owner Practitioner

A year later, one of my friends, Roman who owned a busy practice, offered me a partnership position in his existing firm. He was practicing real estate and entertainment law and his clients wanted his help with litigation. He offered me several of his cases and I came on board as a partner. It was a big decision in my life, but I decided to go into business for myself after three-and-a-half years working for someone else. We formed Gambourg & Borsen LLC, a boutique law firm specializing in corporate transactions, commercial litigation, real estate, entertainment and international law.

Half of my work is commercial litigation while the other half involves corporate transactions. On the litigation side, I do mostly defense work such as partnership disputes. On the transactional side, I formulate corporate documents and create a structure which minimizes potential liability for my clients. In this regard, I act as both a shield and dagger; I shield clients from potential liabilities while asserting their legal rights.

When you run your own practice, you tend to formulate a different kind of trust and relationship with clients. Back when I worked for other law firms, I seldom saw or spoke to clients outside of my office. Now, I receive calls at every hour of the day (and night), on weekends and holidays. I am also proud to say that many of my clients have become very close friends.

Having your own practice also means being exposed to a wide variety of clients and cases. I found that some of my clients would want me to handle all of their cases, knowing some of their requests are outside the scope of my regular practice. As an attorney, you don't want to turn business away, but you never want to provide inadequate representation, it is a delicate balance. I have represented some amazing people many of who I am lucky to call friends.

Success And A Winning Philosophy

In general, I tend to be nice, social and outgoing. I absolutely believe that a favor carries more value than any other form of currency. As such, forming relationships through networking and social interaction are key.

One example which comes to mind has to do with one of my clients who couldn't afford to pay me, so I did the work for free. He turned out to be my greatest source of referrals, which in turn has given me opportunities that opened many doors for my business. It was a simple job, creating an operating agreement between him and his partner, but one that turned into seven years of consistent work.

My Advice To Practitioners

Network. Build relationships. Be nice. I try to be involved in as many things as my plate can hold; you never know who you will meet or who they know. My clients come exclusively from referrals. I have been extremely lucky; I have never had to market my firm. Every attorney can write a memo or draft a motion, but what really separates one attorney from another is their ability to bring in business. Building relationships is the key to success.

Limit Your Billing

I have a rule: I never bill for client communication, i.e. phone calls, quick emails, messages, etc. That's what differentiates me from other attorneys. No other attorney (that I know of) bills like

I do. I never charge for speaking to clients on the phone or meeting clients for a short amount of time. I know it's unusual and most attorneys would not be pleased by me saying so, but charging clients for confiding is illogical to me. This is not to say that work-product driven correspondence and preparatory meetings should not be accounted for but clients should be able to communicate with their counsel without hesitation.

When one charges for every single call or message, two things happen. One, clients will try to limit speaking with you in general. The client will not explain the what, how, and why of their situation without being distracted be their internal ticker. Two, even more important, charging for communication may create a lack of trust. Limiting my billing creates a happy client, one who is eager to share information, which in turn creates a deeper relationship. Indeed, I have a great relationship with my clients, which I credit to the way I conduct my bills.

LOOKING TO THE FUTURE

The whole online research phenomenon occurred prior to me becoming an attorney. I went to law school with those tools in hand. It's not like I experienced the shift of the paradigm between having to look up a case with books and having to look up a case via the Internet. We all see the mountains of books in every attorneys office, but in reality, all one needs is a laptop and an internet connection nowadays.

I do not know where the legal field will go in the future, but the legal system is extremely traditional. In many states you still have to turn in a motion comprised of hundreds if not thousands of pages instead of simply uploading it electronically. As such, I see technological advances develop slower than other industries.

I think many more useful tools could be made available, like an app for WestLawNext or LexisNexis. More so, courts could adopt the federal electronic filing systems which enable most documents to be uploaded on the web.

LIFE BEYOND THE LAW

I am an adjunct professor at Metropolitan College of New York and have been teaching in the Graduate School of Business. I began lecturing traditional classes, such as Business Law and Employment Law. I also instruct MCNY's Constructive Action program. The Constructive Action combines classroom instruction with practical, real world knowledge. It is an exceptional program and one which allows me to work with students inside and outside the classroom.

In following with my family's artistic footsteps, I also invest in Broadway and Music Production. I have been involved with On Golden Pond, Natasha and Pierre and the Great Comet of 1812 and Cosmic Opera.

I also invest in a restaurant called Kitty's Canteen, on the Lower East Side. It serves Jewish and Soul food; the rapper Snoop Dogg is actually an investor. I got into the restaurant business because I represented several restaurants in New York City and naturally, because I like food.

My wife, Morgan, is a doctor of physical therapy and has her own practice, MORE Physio, which caters to outpatient orthopedic injuries. We live in New York City and enjoy all it has to offer.

(This content should be used for informational purposes only. It does not create an attorney-client relationship with any reader and should not be construed as legal advice. If you need legal advice, please contact an attorney in your community who can assess the specifics of your situation.)

10

THE ROAD LESS TRAVELED... DESTINATION: COURTROOM

by Adam T. Dougherty, Esq.

Adam T. Dougherty, Esq.
DOUGHERTY LAW FIRM, P.A.
Deerfield Beach, Florida
www.fl-injurylaw.com

Counselor Dougherty is an AV rated attorney who was born and raised in Cincinnati, Ohio. He graduated from Arizona State University (ASU), earning a B.S. degree in Justice Studies. Prior to practicing law, he worked in law enforcement for over eight years. He graduated from the University of Akron, School of Law and is licensed in all state and federal courts in Arizona and Florida, as well as, the United States Supreme Court. In 2006, he graduated from Gerry Spence's prestigious Trial Lawyers College in Dubois, Wyoming.

In 2015, he was in the first graduating class of the Keenan Ball Trial College in Atlanta, Georgia where he is now on faculty. He lives and practices in Ft. Lauderdale, Florida and runs the DOUGHERTY LAW FIRM, P.A. The firm focuses on plaintiff personal injury. Mr. Dougherty has received numerous awards for his legal ability including: Nations Top One Percent, Top Lawyers of South Florida, Who's Who, South Florida Legal Leaders, and he has a 10.0 AVVO rating.

THE ROAD LESS TRAVELED... DESTINATION: COURTROOM

BEGINNINGS

I was born the last of three boys on December 31, 1970 to Mari Jo and Joseph Dougherty. My mother was born in Cincinnati, Ohio in 1944 and was second generation American. Her father, my grandfather was the son of Italian immigrants and my grandmother's side was British. My father was born in Philadelphia, Pennsylvania in 1942 of Irish decent. My parents met when my father came to Cincinnati on leave from the Navy with his friend and my mom's brother, Frank. They eventually married. My father worked in sales and often multiple jobs to support his wife and three children. He used his GI Bill and put himself through night school and when he graduated from Xavier University he was the first college graduate in his family. My father then began and ran a successful commercial cleaning company for the next 28 years. My mother worked in the travel industry for over 30 years.

My two older brothers, Joe and Patrick, have always helped to keep me in check. As children, neither one of them really wanted much to do with me because of the 3½ and 4½ year age difference from me to them. Joe graduated from high school when I was in seventh grade and then left for Purdue University. Patrick graduated a year later when I was in eighth grade and then took off for the Air Force. Now that we are older, we're all much closer. Truth be told, I can understand why they didn't want their kid brother hanging around them and their friends. As a result I had an active imagination which has stayed with me to this day. I feel blessed to have come from a good family. I have always had a great relationship with my parents, and we have always had an open line of communication. I could always talk to them and ask them for their opinions.

Unlike most of my friends from back home, I delayed getting married until I was 37, and didn't have kids until I was in my forties. My wife, Fabiana is a wonderful woman and my rock. She continues to keep me grounded and I can honestly say that I am a far better man since she entered my life. We were married in her hometown of La Paz, Bolivia in 2008 and since then we have been blessed with two wonderful boys. I absolutely do not regret waiting to start a family. I'm more mature now, and I'm at a point in my life where I can be a better provider and I'm definitely a better husband and father than I would have been in my twenties.

EARLY INFLUENCES

There were so many events and influences in my life. Probably the greatest influence in my life came from my neighborhood. In 1971, my family moved into a new housing development in Forest Park, just North of Cincinnati. The neighborhood was comprised mostly of young families with children. I grew up with so many friends my age it was like an extension of my family and most of us are still close to this day. If I had to pick the most influential person from my neighborhood it would hands down be my next door neighbor, Jim Blair. Jim, may God rest his soul, had a son, Tony who was a year older than me. Jim, imprinted not just on me but other kids in the neighborhood, from about the age of 5 or 6 years old, the dangers of drugs. We heard Jim tell us "say no to drugs" five to ten years before it became a national slogan. Through his persistence and wisdom he saved many of us, not all, from the dangers and heartbreak associated with drug use. For that I will be forever grateful to him.

In 1985, I visited Arizona for the first time. I went out for the summer with a family friend who had moved out there years earlier. After a month my parents and brothers joined me and we traveled throughout the state. It blew me away how different this part of the United States was. It was completely different than anything I had ever been exposed to, the weather, the landscapes, and the people. In Cincinnati, like every other place I had traveled to on the east coast and in the south, everything was fairly black-and-white. Arizona was completely different than anything I had ever experienced. The Latin influence and culture left quite an impression on me. This is why I would later push to go back out west after finishing high school.

Growing up in my neighborhood, I saw people (some older and some my age) who grew up and never left, not even for vacation. Others would go to the same bar and hang out week after week, month after month and year after year. I just couldn't wrap my head around that as a way of life. I wanted more. I wanted to see the world. It was a big decision to pick up and move to Arizona at eighteen years old, just two weeks after graduating from high school, but my parents were supportive in that endeavor. It probably helped that my older brother, Patrick was stationed at Davis-Monthan Air Force Base in Tucson at the time.

In June of 1989, I moved to Tucson, Arizona to follow my dream of becoming a professional baseball player. I enrolled into Pima Community College, then the number one ranked junior college baseball program in the country. I was recruited by coach Rich Alday who helped set me up with a summer team to play on upon my arrival in Tucson. To my dismay, a week before arriving in Tucson, I received a call from Coach Alday informing me he had accepted the head coaching job at the University of New Mexico, a position he would ultimately hold for the next 18 years. What followed was my introduction to the politics of intercollegiate athletics and a subsequent wrist injury that would finally derail my dreams of becoming a pro ballplayer. I wasn't sure what I would do next but I knew that I never wanted to settle for the status quo.

Steps Along The Way - College, Law Enforcement, Brazil & Law School

I was always competitive, but I was far from a stellar student in high school. I kept my grades just good enough to keep me eligible to play sports. When it was time for college I had to reassess my learning habits. Once I realized that my parents and I would eventually be paying for my college, I started to take my studies seriously, and my grades drastically improved. I graduated from Pima Community College in 1992 with an Associate of Applied Science in Criminal Justice and an Associate of Applied Science in Corrections. I then transferred to Arizona State University.

After completing my first semester at Arizona State I took a job with the State of Arizona as a corrections officer working in the juvenile prison. I attempted to carry a part-time university schedule while working as a corrections officer, and that was a disaster. I put my studies on hold. After a few years of working in the institution, I took a job as a Parole Officer III. I was the only parole officer in Pinal County, a rural county which covered 5,200 square miles between Phoenix and Tucson. I set my own hours and my own schedule, allowing me the flexibility to return to Arizona State and finish my Bachelors of Science in Justice Studies.

My decision to go to law school was an interesting one that came later. While working as a Parole Officer, I began to have frequent interactions with attorneys (both county attorneys and criminal defense attorneys). I had always heard from other people how hard it was to get through law school as well as the horror stories of the bar exam, the challenge intrigued me. I looked at some of the attorneys I was having contact with and thought, "If they can get through law school, I can do it too." I knew I underachieved in high school and college and in the back of my mind I knew if I applied myself I could do it. I decided to go for it. Upon re-enrolling into Arizona State I applied myself and made the dean's list every semester through graduation.

After graduation I took the LSAT and started to send out my applications to different law schools. At the same time I was applying for law schools, I was finishing up a nearly two year process of testing and interviewing with the U.S. Customs Service. In June of 1999, I received a phone call from the U.S. Customs Service congratulating me on successfully completing the hiring process and offering me a job as a Customs Inspector, at the Port of Los Angeles earning a G5 salary. I remember saying, "but I qualified as a GS7?" The person on the other end promptly responded that while I qualified for a GS7 position, I was being offered the job as a GS5. The answer to my next question floored me. "What is the pay for a GS5?" The person on the other line responded, "At that location, Port of Los Angeles it's $23,500.00 plus shift differential." My jaw dropped, I kindly explained that I was not in a position to take a more than $15,000.00 pay cut to move to Los Angeles where the cost of living was significantly higher. I turned down the job offer, even though I'd really wanted to work for the Feds. The person on the other line couldn't believe it; I don't think that many people have told them 'no' after going through that process and finally being offered a job. I wasn't everybody else. My mind was now made up, I was going to go to law school.

I applied and was accepted into the University of Dayton and I was set to enroll in the fall of 1999. Prior to leaving for law school, in July of 1999, I traveled to Brazil for a month to train and compete in the 1999 World Jiu-Jitsu Championships. This was my first time leaving the country for an extended period of time (I had many border crossings into Sonora, Mexico as an undergrad). Like my first trip to Arizona as a fourteen year old... this was an eye opening and life changing experience and I relished it. I met many wonderful people and more than a few of them have become dear, lifelong friends!

Upon my return to the United States I promptly called the University of Dayton and asked to delay my enrollment until the fall of 2000. They happily obliged. On the invitation of some of my new Brazilian friends (who later became like brothers) I returned to Brazil to spend another three months training jiu-jitsu at Gracie Tijuca and Humaita and learning Portuguese.

Upon my return from Brazil, I applied to a few new law schools but I really wanted to get into my Alma Mater, Arizona State University. After a few months passed, the moment I was waiting for finally arrived, a letter from the Arizona State University

School of Law… I was put on the waiting list! I couldn't believe it. Two days later, I received a phone call from the University of Akron congratulating me on being a Millennium Scholar and informing me my first year of law school was paid for minus books and taxes. I was off to Ohio.

Since I had deferred law school for a year, I was now anxious to tackle the challenge of getting through law school. I returned to Arizona in the summers and took full-time classes at Arizona State. In May of 2002, after finishing my second year of law school at Akron, I got a job working part-time for Comair, a former subsidiary of Delta Airlines. My brother Joe was working for Delta at the time and I envied his free flight benefits. I wanted the free flight benefits because I wanted to travel and see the world… for free. My final semester of law school was in the fall of 2002, I had successfully graduated from law school in 2½ years. It was now time to study for and take the bar exam. I promptly gathered all of my bar study materials and to the dismay of my friends and parents informed them I was heading to Rio de Janeiro for three weeks to study for the Florida Bar Exam. Everyone thought I was crazy. It was a bold move but it paid off. In February of 2003, I sat for and passed the Florida Bar Exam. A celebratory flight to London followed… got to love those free flight benefits. In the nearly three years I spent with Comair I flew over five hundred thousand miles and went back and forth to Europe and South America with great frequency.

On October 31, 2003, I moved to Florida. I had successfully passed the bar exam but had not yet applied to the Florida Bar. I wanted to wait until I settled down in Florida. I took a job with the Broward County Sheriff's Office as an administrator in the jail supervising the Confinement Status Unit. In December of 2003, I submitted my application to the Florida Bar which they quickly processed. On March 18, 2004, I took my oath for the Florida Bar.

PRACTICE OF LAW – A TRIAL LAWYER EMERGES

Soon after receiving my law license, I sent my application to the Broward County State Attorney's Office. It just so happened that the person in charge of hiring was in the process of retiring, so no one got back with me. I knew a young lady, Rachel Maldanado who worked at the Public Defender's Office and one day she asked me, "Why don't you give your application to the Public Defender's Office?" I hadn't even thought about it. She said, "Give me your application. I'm going take it over." I gave it to her, and didn't think much about it.

The next day, I got a call from Alan Schreiber, the elected Public Defender, who said, "Come on over and talk to me." After meeting with him for about two hours, he offered me a job as an Assistant Public Defender, I was ready to practice law, so I accepted it. Two weeks into that job, I received a call from the Broward Sheriff's Office Legal Department (who knew I received my law license and expressed their interest in having me). They had just received the approval to bring me on board. They said, "We called your desk at your old position, and were told you left two weeks ago to go to the Public Defender's Office. We just got approval for this position, and we'd like for you to come work for us." I was extremely flattered. I responded, "Thank you very much, but you're two weeks too late, and I've already given my word, already given my commitment, and I don't want to start burning bridges. Thank you again, but the timing just wasn't right." The hiring attorney understood and commended me for keeping my commitment. The sheriff's office job paid significantly more money but money isn't everything.

I'll never forget the night before my first day on the job. I actually called my old criminal law professor at the University of Akron, a wonderful instructor by the name of Dana Cole, who is also on staff at Gerry Spence Trial Lawyer's College in Wyoming. I said, "Dana, how am I going to do this? I've worked in law enforcement for the last 8 years." Dana basically told me "It's a constitutional right and everybody has that right. Go in there and make sure that the police did their job, no one cut corners, no one lied, and no one cheated. That's what you're going to do." He was right, and that's what I've done ever since.

At the Public Defender's Office I was fortunate enough to be surrounded by some phenomenal attorneys, including my mentor, H. Dohn Williams. At that time, the Public Defender's Office under Mr. Schreiber's guidance was a breeding ground for up and coming, highly talented trial lawyers. Under Al's administration, Assistant Public Defenders were encouraged to file and argue motions and most importantly... try cases! I handled thousands of felony cases and tried numerous felony cases including two first degree murder cases. The learning experience I received from that office has proven invaluable.

In 2006, I was honored to be one of 55 attorneys in the United States selected to attend Gerry Spence's Trial Lawyers College in Dubois, Wyoming. It is an intensive work filled three weeks on his ranch, working and training with the best trial attorneys and consultants in the country. That college definitely had huge influence on my legal career, and taught me that I wanted to be the best trial attorney that I could be. Having firsthand interaction and instruction from the likes of Gerry Spence, Paul Luvera, Jim Fitzgerald and Josh Karton among others helped my trial skills immeasurably. The ranch was comprised of an All-Star line-up of this country's greatest trial lawyers. Not only did it make me a better attorney, it made me hungry.

MY PHILOSOPHY OF SUCCESS

A lot of people define success with material things they are able to accumulate: money, expensive cars, big houses, etc. I on the other hand don't think that way.

My philosophy of success centers on being the best person that I can be. I have to constantly look in the mirror and evaluate myself in all aspects of my life. Am I the best husband, father, brother, or son that I can be? Am I the best attorney that I can be? What makes me a good attorney? Is it the amount of money I earn or how well I represent my clients? Is it how I fight for them? Do I do the best that I can every day? Can I look in the mirror at the end of the day, knowing that I did my best for my clients?

This may come as a surprise to most, but I believe one of the most essential ingredients to success is failure. You will learn more from your mistakes and failures than you will ever learn from your victories. Failure makes you reflect and self-analyze. Failure makes you hungry. The ability to learn from your mistakes and turn stumbling blocks into stepping stones leads to success.

It is my belief that if you take care of your business in a professional and personal way, then success will come, in your finances, your practice, and in your life. No one can be successful at anything unless they invest time and energy into it. So, you've got to reflect. You can be a terrible husband and father, and a successful attorney, if you only devote your life to the law. You can be a wonderful husband and father, and be a terrible attorney, if you only devote time to your family. Finding that balance requires self-evaluation, reflection and if you're married, a great and understanding spouse.

Becoming successful on a number of levels requires a lot of time, energy, and commitment to follow through on all the things necessary to your journey. I think, if you have a solid moral core, along with good values, and you do the right thing for the right reasons, then you will be successful. If you try to take shortcuts, those shortcuts will only lead to trouble.

I know plenty of attorneys who base success on the number of cases they have, and the amount of money they've made. Some of these attorneys will accumulate both, yet sacrifice other things, from their morals to their quality of work. Many attorneys aim at having huge caseloads, because they never know when their next case will arrive, but if you get to the point of having too many cases, you can't possibly dedicate your time and energy in the way that those cases deserve. Not only are you cheating yourself, more importantly, you're cheating your clients. You need to find balance, in life, in family and in work.

THE FUTURE OF MY PROFESSION

I believe the future of my profession is headed for continued rough times. Over the last 25-30 years, lawyers in general, and trial attorneys specifically have been vilified. Why is that? Because politicians, big companies, the insurance industry and the American Medical Association has told you we're bad. It is quite ironic, since no one trusts politicians in the first place. Not one election goes by that you don't hear, "medical bills are high because of these trial lawyers. Things you buy are high-priced because of these trial lawyers and, your insurance premiums are high because of trial lawyers." Politicians are funded by the big money of insurance companies, the Chambers of Commerce, and the deep pockets of the American Medical Association.

I am proud of the fact I am a trial attorney. Have you ever stopped to ask yourself why trial lawyers have been vilified? Forget what you heard in the media. Tort reform and jackpot justice have been imbedded in the average American's psyche over the last 25-30 years by the above named bad actors for a reason. What is that reason? It's simple. *We hold bad actors responsible!* To the public's detriment, the tort reform campaign has skewed the image of trial attorneys into the equivalent of the bogeyman. Insurance companies don't want you to know they are making record profits and their first obligation is to their shareholders and not their policy holders. Drug companies and manufacturing companies don't want you to know they brought a product to market too soon before they had enough information over time to see if a drug or product was really safe. Manufacturing companies don't want you to know that a decision was made in a board room wherein they knew a product they manufactured was unsafe and could result in serious injury or death but that it would be more cost effective to payout wrongful death claims instead of recalling a dangerous product. The American Medical Association would rather protect incompetent member doctors and complain that their malpractice insurance premiums are too high for them to offer effective medical services.

To prove the point, look back to this past December the manufactures of hover-boards were racing to get their products to market in time for the holiday shopping season… and they did. Then in January of this year these things were catching fire and blowing up all over the world on a daily basis. There is now a massive global recall. People have been burned and seriously injured as a result of corporate *GREED*. Somehow I'm sure they will try and blame these defective products on the trial lawyers. Trial lawyers have been vilified over money. Money these companies have to spend to compensate their victims. You will also see these same companies vilify the attorney's "fees." They will say that the attorneys in these cases often get all the money and the clients get little to nothing. This is like pouring salt into a wound they have caused. These companies know very well that most people cannot afford to pay an attorney $350 to $500 an hour to take their case. That is why lawyers offer contingent fee agreements with clients. The client does not have to come up with any money up front and the attorney gets paid "only if" he wins the case. It is the attorney that fronts all of the money to bring the case. The amount of money the attorney spends can range from hundreds of dollars to millions of dollars.

These companies cause the problems that injure consumers then blame the "trial lawyers" because they, the company, failed to do the right thing in the first place. Let's be clear: if insurance companies and other big manufacturing companies conducted themselves honestly… there would be no need for trial attorneys.

Most people don't realize that lawyers are doctors too. We get *juris doctorate* degrees or doctor of jurisprudence degrees, but in the United States no one refers to us or calls us "doctor." My wife is from South America. Whenever I'm fortunate enough to travel through the Caribbean, Central America, or South America, I am often addressed by people as "Doctor." At first it was weird to hear, but let me be clear, it is done as a show of respect. In most of the rest of the world, people have a great respect for attorneys and the legal profession. The respect comes from the fact that a lawyer has sacrificed and spent a significant amount of time to go to school and get a license to practice. In the United States, it's the polar opposite - lawyers are viewed as ambulance chasers, liars, cheaters, and opportunists. It's sad, what politicians and the whole tort reform movement have done to a very prestigious profession. Twenty-five of our forty-four presidents were attorneys. In the end though, it will be the average person who suffers because of this.

For anyone who has not seen the 2011 documentary *Hot Coffee* directed by Susan Saladoff, I highly suggest you watch it. It does more justice to this concerning issue than my short take. Ms. Saladoff's documentary goes through four phases: the McDonald's hot coffee case, tort reform, judicial reform, and arbitration. She does an excellent job explaining the origins of tort reform, from big tobacco and Karl Rove through judicial reform and how the chamber of commerce is dumping millions of dollars into judicial campaigns so that they can elect appellate judges that will be favorable to big corporations (in turn those judges would reverse big verdicts). Finally, the end of the documentary discusses people unknowingly giving away their rights. For instance, you can't even sign up for a credit card without agreeing to a three-person panel of arbitration, which means you've signed away your right to judicial intervention if you need to sue a credit card company. These companies constantly deal in disputes and pick and pay arbitrators leaving the average person on an island. How fair do you think these arbitrators will be to your plight when they deal daily and are paid daily by the company on the other side? That is why I think the direction we're headed is a very scary one.

BECOMING A LEADER

Attorneys have the reputation for being "know it alls." It's a stereotype that our profession breeds because many of us have an unwillingness to admit we are wrong or don't know something.

Attorneys like that are lying to themselves. A good attorney realizes that he doesn't know everything. A great attorney realizes the dynamics of the profession in this country are changing and to stay on top you can't just sit back and settle for the old way of doing things. Excellent attorneys are constantly re-educating themselves, learning new methods and practicing the skills that will make them the leaders in their field. Attorneys that fail to evolve do themselves and their clients a disfavor. Leaders don't settle for the status quo, they have an interest in bettering themselves and honing their craft and work hard to get where they are.

As a personal injury attorney, I've had to learn medical jargon because, eventually, I have to explain it to an adjuster or if it goes to trial, to six jurors. I have to know the medicine and human anatomy and be able to explain that knowledge in everyday language so that ordinary people can understand it. If the jurors you are trying your case in front of don't understand you or what you're trying to get across to them, you'll *NEVER* win your case!

Humility is another trait that many attorneys lack. Attorneys are people to, and we're vulnerable to mistakes. Having confidence is great but when we look and talk down to people it defeats our purpose and feeds in to the negative stereotypes people have about us.

Probably the biggest mistake we attorneys make is we don't always listen to our clients. It is amazing what you can learn if you just stop talking and listen to what your client has to say.

THE BIGGEST CHALLENGES ATTORNEYS FACE

I've already touched on a couple of the challenges, tort reform, and the public's perception of lawyers.

People make fun of attorneys and mock them, until they actually need one. When they need an attorney and have to deal with one, they understand that the law is really serious. When they see the forces stacked up against them on the other side, be it the government, big insurance or big corporations and all the money that gets spent to defeat them, the average person finally realizes the uphill battle they face.

Advertising is the third huge challenge for attorneys. It's a big deal, and it's hard for the solo practitioners and the small firms to compete against the mega firms that are popping up everywhere. Some of these law firms drop tens of millions of dollars into advertising! I feel for the average person who doesn't need an attorney on a daily basis. When they do need one, they have to decide who to pick. It's easy for those people who find themselves in sudden need to fall back on ads they see plastered all over billboards, taxi cabs, and their TV. There is something to be said for advertising, but mostly it creates an unequal playing field and it doesn't insure that your attorney knows what they're doing. That's not to say that some of those mega firms don't have some really phenomenal lawyers working for them, they do. They also have some very bad lawyers working for them so again, you never know unless you ask.

WHY YOU SHOULD HIRE AN ATTORNEY

It is important for people to know their rights. They also need to consult with someone who will explain the process to them, which can be very confusing. I tell all my clients when they hire me my job is two-fold. Number one, I am their mouthpiece – my job is to tell their story, first to the insurance adjusters and then, if necessary, to the jury. My second job is to give my clients legal advice, and explain to them how certain factors will affect their case.

Most clients have misconceptions about the legal process in general. Their knowledge often comes from television, movies or books. For example, when a client comes in to be prepared for a deposition, they think it's time for me to tell them what they need to say. I then explain to them the process doesn't work that way. When I prepare my client for a deposition, it's a long process that is often spread over three days, sometimes more. As an attorney, it's not my job to tell my client what to say, but rather help them find their own voice so that they can tell their own story. As for settlement offers, I will tell them if I think an offer is fair, but ultimately it is the client's decision to accept it or not. Another part of what I do is to sort through unrealistic expectations. As attorneys, we have to be able to explain things effectively to our clients and manage their expectations.

When choosing an attorney to represent your interest, people should keep one important thing in mind, the attorney's ability to get you justice. An analogy I like to use is: "not all doctors are surgeons, just like not all attorneys are trial lawyers." A personal injury attorney or law firm that does not try cases is not going to get you full compensation. The insurance companies know what attorneys and law firms try cases and which ones don't. The ones that don't try cases, settle cases for less. Why? Because, insurance companies are in the business of managing risks. What risk is there to the insurance company that low balls an attorney or law firm that does not go to court? Answer: none. On the flip side, attorneys and law firms that do try cases can make insurance companies pay significantly more, and at times, in excess of their policy limits.

To be able to walk into a courtroom and think on your feet, react to changing arguments, react to judicial decisions with which you may, or may not, agree, puts you in a much different place than an attorney that sits behind his desk. An attorney who never walks into a courtroom doesn't have to put himself out there in front of God, country, mother, and everyone else. Being a trial lawyer means you possess a skill set that's equivalent to that of doctors who actually do surgery and not just consultations with patients. It is my belief that being a trial lawyer puts you in a better position to obtain fair compensation for your clients.

INNOCENT UNTIL PROVEN GUILTY

Although I focus most of my cases these days on personal injury, I still take a few criminal cases every year. Criminal defense attorneys are often asked how they can represent someone they know is guilty? The answer, while confusing to some, it is quite simple, it's a constitutional right. Before this country was founded and the constitution was written, there was an infamous event known as the Boston Massacre. John Adams, our second President, represented those British soldiers involved in the Boston Massacre. That didn't make him a very popular attorney in Boston in the eighteenth century, but he defended those soldiers because the Rule of Law demanded it. Our laws still depend on the Rule of Law today. Now that we have the Constitution, everyone has a constitutional right to a defense, and a right to face their accusers. Imagine what it would be like if we didn't protect the rights of criminals? How long would it take for someone to be falsely accused as being a criminal? Then innocent people accused of crimes would have no rights. When you protect the rights of the least among us, everyone is protected. It is a system that keeps the balance.

In my opinion, it is far easier to represent a guilty client than an innocent one. A client that is guilty who has his day in court and is found guilty, I can live with that. When you represent a client that is innocent, the pressure and stress can become immeasurable. The stakes are never higher than when an innocent person is facing the loss of liberty.

IMPORTANT QUALITIES OF TOP ATTORNEYS

An attorney must be a problem solver. I've been supervising people, and empowering them to be problem solvers, for over 20 years. I tell all of my staff that I have an open door policy, but I also constantly say, "Don't just bring me problems; bring me solutions." That relates back to realizing that you don't know everything. If I can empower a paralegal, or a case manager, to come up with a better way of doing something, then I'm willing to listen. Ideas generate creativity and production, and I realize that I may not have all the best ideas. A really good attorney must be willing to listen to the people around him or her.

Use the power of goal setting. Without goals, what are you working towards? Once you set goals, ask yourself if they are the right goals? It is extremely important to know where you want to go, but you need to have a plan and a process to get you there.

Be willing to pay the price by putting in the hard work and sacrifice necessary to accomplish your goals. Anything that has real worth is not easy to get. I did not want to leave Arizona to go to law school in Akron, Ohio, but that was the price I had to pay. Engage in constant, never-ending self-improvement. When I go into Barnes and Nobles or another big bookstore, I always find myself wandering into the self-improvement area and looking at new topics and ideas on the shelves. In my core, I want to keep growing and learning new things.

In 2010 I met one of this country's best attorneys, Don Keenan in Atlanta, GA. Don, a member of the Inner Circle of Advocates, co-authored a book with Dr. David Ball, a jury consultant, titled: *Reptile: The 2009 Manual of the Plantiff's Revolution.* That book gave attorneys new insight on how to present cases and combat the influences of tort reform. In May of 2015, I was in the first graduating class of the Keenan Ball Trial College (KBC) in Atlanta, Georgia. If you do insurance defense work or corporate defense work you are ineligible to attend. I am now honored to be on faculty at the KBC. It affords me the opportunity to be around some of the best attorneys in the country on a routine basis.

It is easy for attorneys that work day in and day out, to have their fires start to burn slow. However, programs like the Gerry Spence's Trial Lawyers College and the Keenan Ball Trial College put attorneys in a position of interacting and listening to some of the best attorneys in the country. Through this self-betterment process attorneys learn new concepts and find out what other attorneys are doing in their practices that you're not. It is incredibly motivating and re-stokes the flame and gets the fire burning again.

Another important quality of being a top attorney is exceeding people's expectations. My motto is this: I would rather under-promise, and over-deliver to my clients every single time. If I do that, every single one of my clients will be happy. When you over-promise, and under-deliver, you will start developing problems.

WHY YOU SHOULD HIRE A PERSONAL INJURY ATTORNEY

The average person is no match for an insurance company's money or experience, while an attorney will know the value of cases and can get more money for their clients.

Before getting into the dynamics of insurance companies and their adversarial position, let's talk about the McKinsey & Company. The company was founded in 1926 and is the world's most successful strategic consulting firm, and consults with most of the Fortune 100 companies. In 1992, the company was asked to take a look at Allstate Insurance; in doing so, they dramatically changed the way that insurance companies adjudicated their injury claims. In their studies, the McKinsey Global Institute found that injured claimants who hired an attorney were getting settlements at five times the size of unrepresented claimants.

In 1992, McKinsey basically sold Allstate a top-to-bottom redesign that would take years to implement. This brand-new problem-solving tool was redesigned to have Allstate change their claims handling process for the sole purpose of increasing shareholder value and net profit. Essentially, they attacked the way Allstate was processing their claims for bodily injuries and uninsured motorists based on "Subjective Injuries." McKinsey stressed to Allstate that as a publicly held corporation of shareholders, their duty was to make a profit for their shareholders, even at the expense of their policy holders.

In the mid 1990's, Allstate implemented the suggestions of McKinsey and turned from "good hands to boxing gloves" in an effort to start cutting claims by five to 15 percent. If you want more information on how McKinsey and Allstate changed the claims handling business read, *From Good Hands to Boxing Gloves: The Dark Side of Insurance* by David Berardinelli.

Even though we all have to buy insurance, people have no idea insurance companies are making record profits. It is impossible in this country to watch a major sporting event without seeing an insurance advertisement. I ask clients, "Why do you think they made you no offer or this insulting low offer? Because they're spending the millions of dollars on advertising, instead of fairly settling their injury claims for what they are worth." During the next football or basketball game you watch on T.V., just count the number of expensive, 30-second car insurance commercials you see. These are the main reasons that people are having their claims delayed, denied, and defended by the insurance companies.

LANDMINES AND PERSONAL INJURY CASES

It is extremely important for clients that are injured be honest with their attorneys. If a client has a prior accident or prior injury they have to inform their attorney so that the attorney can navigate around it and deal with it ahead of time. Once a bomb goes off, an attorney can't do anything about it. Once a client has tripped the bomb and it's blown up because they weren't candid with their attorney, there's nothing that can be done about it. Before I put a case into litigation, I pull all of my clients back in to meet with me and we talk about everything.

People don't realize it but insurance companies have all the money and information in the world, at their fingertips. Insurance companies share claims information with one another; each company can see the updated claim history of any claimant's property damage, or injury claims. Nothing hurts your case worse than lying to your attorney or not telling them about an accident where they claimed prior injuries. When the attorney works up the case and sends in the demand, it's not a good surprise to hear an adjuster say, "please send me the information from the 2010 crash." Client honesty is essential.

Earlier in my career, I represented a retired police officer who decided to retire in Florida. This client had slipped and fell in a supermarket in standing water that was allowed to stay on the floor. The client was taken by a trauma helicopter to the nearest big city with a level one trauma center. This client spent the next 2 weeks in the hospital with very serious injuries. It was clear this was going to be a big case. The EMTs that responded reported they found my client on the scene in a puddle of water and it was the direct cause of the injuries. The case went into litigation. As a former police officer, the client had been deposed hundreds of times. When it came time to prepare the client for deposition the client wanted to rush through the preparation process. My final instructions to the client were, "tell the truth, only answer the question being asked and if you honestly don't know the answer to a question say, 'I don't know', don't guess or say what you think they want to hear." The deposition appeared to go very well. Afterwards the defense attorney said to me, "Your client made a great witness let me talk to my carrier, the only question now is how much."

What happened next was devastating. The defense attorney, on orders from the insurance carrier subpoenaed my client's employment file from the former out of state police department. When the records arrived it showed the client had a worker's compensation claim for an injury to his neck and shoulder. As a result of that claim, the client was unable to draw their duty weapon and was given a desk assignment. For that injury the client received treatment for both neck and shoulder complaints with an orthopedic surgeon. Why is that relevant? Because in the client's deposition the following three questions were asked:

1. Have you ever injured your neck or received medical treatment for your neck?

2. Have you ever injured your shoulder or received medical treatment for your shoulder?

3. Have you ever consulted or been treated by an orthopedic surgeon?

My client had answered "no" to all 3 questions. In this case, the facts were clear, my client was severely injured and the supermarket was clearly liable. Had my client been honest with me and not lied, the prior worker's compensation claim, in my belief, would have had little to no effect on this claim. Because of the lie, the court dismissed the lawsuit for fraud upon the court.

UM/UIM COVERAGE

Everyone should have a UM (uninsured motorist) or UIM under-insured motorist) policy with enough coverage to protect them. If your state differentiates between the two types, get both. UM and UIM coverage protects you when (a) someone without insurance hits you or (b) someone that doesn't have enough bodily insurance coverage to cover your losses hits you, then your insurance (through your UM/UIM policy) will stand in the place of the person who hurt you. God forbid that you are so seriously injured after a motor vehicle crash that you need a surgery and the person that hit you has little or no Bodily Injury coverage and you did not have UM or UIM coverage.

While UM insurance will increase your policy's premium, it is not that much more expensive. I recall getting an auto insurance quote in my twenties, when I saw the premium for six months I remember asking if there any way to lower it? The immediate suggestion I received from my agent was to get rid of the UM coverage which would save me money on my premium. By canceling the UM coverage, the insurance company knows they will not be on the hook if you're involved in a bad accident.

FLORIDA'S FAILURE TO PROTECT TOURISTS & THEIR CITIZENS

One of the terrible things about living in the State of Florida is that we are the *ONLY* state in the country that *DOES NOT REQUIRE* drivers to carry minimum bodily injury coverage. For a list of state by state requirements visit: http://www.nerdwal let.com/blog/insurance/car-insurance/. While some states require their drivers to purchase both bodily injury and uninsured motorist coverage, Florida only requires drivers to carry Personal Injury Protection (PIP) coverage and Property Damage. Both coverages are required at a minimum limit of $10,000.00. Since Florida is a no-fault state, by law, if someone injures you as a result of a car accident, your car insurance MUST cover the first $10,000 of your medical bills. However, that $10,000.00 will be capped at $2,500.00 unless a doctor opines you have sustained an emergency medical condition as a result of the accident. The PIP coverage also becomes primary over your health insurance, mandating that you use your PIP benefits first.

Florida's failure to mandate minimum bodily injury coverage is disgraceful and the members of the Florida legislature should be ashamed of themselves. Florida is one of the world's top tourist destinations and our legislature is the only one in the country that doesn't require people who drive on our roads to maintain a minimum bodily injury policy. I have had four separate death cases in which I have had to tell family members, "I'm sorry, there's nothing I can do for you" because the party responsible for the death did not have Bodily Injury Coverage, and the deceased did not have a UM policy. There is no worse feeling than telling someone grieving the loss of a loved one, you can't help them and there is no means of compensation available to them. Sure, the family can go after the person individually, but someone driving without insurance more than likely doesn't have any money. There are not many attorneys willing to go get a paper judgment that they will never be able to collect on. In my career, I have only gone after one such person. That person happened to be former NFL football player, Plaxico Burress. He had just signed a five year $30 million dollar contract with the New York Giants so me and the firm I worked for at the time felt comfortable we would be able to collect.

TRUCKING ACCIDENTS ARE NOT LIKE MOTOR VEHICLE ACCIDENTS

Unfortunately, around 95% of personal injury attorneys who take on clients with truck accident cases treat the case like a motor vehicle accident. By doing that, these attorneys costs their clients upwards of hundreds of thousands of dollars. If you or a family member has been involved in a crash with a tractor-trailer (18-wheeler, Semi), be careful in choosing an attorney. If your attorney is not a member of the Association of Plaintiff Interstate Trucking Lawyers of America (APITLA), don't sign up with them. These cases are completely different from motor vehicle cases and most are guided by the Federal Motor Carrier Safety Regulations (FMCSR). The FMCSR was implemented by Congress and there are specific things that drivers and truck companies must comply with. In addition, the FMCSR lays out specific time frames for document retention, drug testing and other things. An attorney not familiar with this area of law can unintentionally and dramatically devalue your case preventing you from obtaining the compensation you deserve.

I worked for a big advertising law firm that sometimes obtained these cases. By the time the case ended up on my desk to be litigated, it had been terribly mismanaged by a pre-suit attorney. This particular pre-suit attorney handling the file was completely unfamiliar with the FMCSR and didn't know how to implement essential protocols that needed to take place immediately after the crash: i.e. spoliation letters to the trucking company, hiring a trucking expert, etc. The damage done by this pre-suit attorney was significant and it cost my former client a significant amount of money.

ADVANTAGES OF SMALL VS. LARGE LAW FIRMS

My small boutique firm affords me the opportunity to meet with my clients, get to know them and work on their cases. One of the dangers of the giant personal injury mills is that client's will probably only meet with a partner when it's time to sign up their case. Some client's will never meet the partner. After the sign up is complete your case will then be passed around from associate attorney to associate attorney, which I find always upsets the client. One of the biggest complaints I heard from former client's when I worked at a large advertised firm was, "you're the fourth attorney on my case, what happened to Mr. / Ms. X?"

Most big firms also separate their cases and attorneys into a pre-suit department and litigation department. It's not uncommon for a case to languish in the pre-suit department for a couple of years before it's transferred to the litigation department. Then the litigating attorney (who actually knows the rules of law) will review the case and prepare it for litigation. More often than not the litigating attorney is trying to clean up the pre-suit attorneys mess. Maybe there was a witness that has never been contacted, maybe someone never went out and took photographs of the scene, maybe spoliation letters that could have preserved evidence never went out and now that evidence is gone. Those were some of my biggest frustrations when I worked with the bigger law firms.

Clients like to know who they are dealing with. Running a small boutique law firm assures clients that I am actually the one handling their case.

BAD FAITH LAWS — A WARNING

There's a lot of talk in the state legislatures about banning or getting rid of 'bad faith' laws against insurance companies. If this happens, it will be the people who suffer. *BAD FAITH LAWS ARE THE ONLY LINE OF PROTECTION PEOPLE HAVE AGAINST THE INSURANCE COMPANIES!* As I discussed earlier about tort reform and judicial reform, people need to understand that insurance companies and the various chambers of commerce are paying billions of dollars to influence politicians and voters to do away with 'bad faith' laws. Politicians will try and tell voters that bad faith laws are bad and that these laws are the reason for skyrocketing insurance rates. This is all untrue, you can read for yourself: http://www.citizen.org/congress/article_redirect.cfm? ID=9008. In fact, those states that have passed these laws and other tort reform laws have not seen any drop in insurance premiums! This is what bad faith means: if an insurance company could have or should have settled a claim for fair compensation, and they didn't, they are operating in bad faith.

For example, let's say Mr. Doe gets rear-ended and needs to have multiple spinal surgeries; the at-fault person who rear-ended him only has a $100,000 policy. Mr. Doe's doctors tell him that he's going to need these surgeries, and that information is sent to the insurance company. That information also shows that the surgery and post-surgical rehabilitation will cost more than the at-fault party's policy limits of $100,000. At that point, the insurance company should evaluate the case and tender their policy limits of $100,000.

In a recent case of mine, one of the major advertising insurance companies decided not to be a good neighbor and offered my client a ridiculous $5,000 to settle their claim, this even after they saw that my client was a candidate for a lumbar fusion surgery. This insurance company knew that the claim was valued at far more than that. The client elected to have the surgery and the case was put into litigation. The insurance company made my client wait nearly two years to be compensated all the while the client's credit was taking a beating for unpaid medical bills. In the end, the at-fault party's insurance paid over the initial policy limits of $500,000 to settle the case.

The scary part is, if state legislatures get rid of the bad faith laws they will essentially be removing the guillotine hanging over the heads of the insurance companies. By removing bad faith laws, the worst thing that could happen to an insurance company is they would be forced to pay the policy limits. Since that's the worst thing that could happen, paying the limits, why then would insurance companies ever offer fair value to settle a claim? The bad faith laws are the only checks and balances the consumers have against the insurance companies. Insurance companies would never be found to be in "bad faith" if they engaged in fair negotiations and settlements.

Medical malpractice reforms (another form of tort reform), was passed in some states by enraging the people about the soaring costs of medical/health insurance. After the dust settled, the passage of tort reform had the opposite effect and those states actually showed the highest increase of medical/health insurance premiums and malpractice insurance. A simple Google search on tort reform and its affect on insurance premiums will give you a treasure trove of studies and comments from insurance companies disproving the link between tort reform and lower insurance premiums.

People also think that damage caps are good because they'll deter frivolous lawsuits, but damage caps sometimes keep people from getting the care they need after an accident. The public needs to be educated on both sides. As Americans, we give up our rights every day without realizing it. If I could just get people to understand that their politicians and the government in general have sold them a lie with tort reform, I would consider that a success.

WORDS OF WISDOM

Surrounding yourself with positive people is a must – it's crucial in life and in business. Negative people and bad attitudes are like a cancer and can quickly destroy an office environment. Negative people create unnecessary chaos. Once it starts, it spreads rapidly. When you have good people, pay them, do what you have to do to keep them around, because good help is hard to find. Your employees will either set your ship to sail, or sink it.

Embrace change. Otherwise, you will struggle to be successful. Attorneys who are trying cases the same way they did 20 or 30 years ago are probably not having the success they used to because everything has changed.

Create a daily to-do list. In fact, I've mandated all of my staff to make one. I've told them that I want to see their to-do list because, otherwise, they will just get caught up in the fast-moving environment of telephone calls, constant emails, etc. It's easy to get off-track, the to-do-list gives you to something to fall back on. If you don't have a list, you'll forget something as you move on to the next five things, so that you never complete your essential tasks for that day.

Lastly, and most importantly, make your clients feel comfortable with you, and confident in you. Don't just ask questions of them - listen to their answers. Talk to them and you will be amazed at some of the things you can learn about them that can help you with their case.

Keep it simple, work hard, play hard and enjoy all life has to offer. Maintain your integrity and values and every chance you get, love those around you! Do this and you will have led a successful life!

(This content should be used for informational purposes only. It does not create an attorney-client relationship with any reader and should not be construed as legal advice. If you need legal advice, please contact an attorney in your community who can assess the specifics of your situation.)

www.ingramcontent.com/pod-product-compliance
Lightning Source LLC
Chambersburg PA
CBHW070308200326
41518CB00010B/1929